BRITISH COASTAL SHIPS
TUGS AND TRAWLERS

BRITISH
Coastal Ships
TUGS AND TRAWLERS

D. RIDLEY CHESTERTON

LONDON

IAN ALLAN

First published 1972

SBN 7110 0313 0

© Ian Allan 1972

*Published by Ian Allan Ltd, Shepperton, Surrey, and printed in the United
Kingdom by The Press at Coombelands Ltd, Addlestone, Surrey.*

Contents

Abbreviations

General

M=Diesel or I.C. engines
ME=As above, but with electric drive
RT=Combined steam reciprocating and turbine machinery
SR=Steam reciprocating, compound or triple expansion
ST=Steam turbines
TE=Steam turbines with electric drive

(A)=Engines aft
(2) (3) etc. Twin-screw, Triple-screw
(PW)=Paddle wheel
(B)=Brake or Shaft Horse Power
(I)=Indicated Horse Power (Usually reckoned as 87% of B.H.P.)
(D)=Displacement Tonnage

In Tug Section

FF=Fitted with Fire-Fighting Equipment
KN=Kort Nozzle
Pshr=Pusher Tug
Salv=Salvage Tug
VS=Voith-Schneider Screw

Trawler Port Registry Letters

All fishing vessels bear Port Registry letters and numbers near the bows and often on some other part as well. Identification is simplified by the inclusion of these in the text, where the following will be found:

A=Aberdeen	**GY**=Grimsby	**LT**=Lowestoft
BCK=Buckie	**HL**=Hartlepool	**M**=Milford Haven
FD=Fleetwood	**H**=Hull	**PZ**=Penzance (Newlyn)
GN=Granton	**LH**=Leith	**SN**=North Shields
GW=Glasgow	**LO**=London	**YH**=Yarmouth

Note on Description of Funnel and Hull Colours

In describing funnel and hull colours, terms such as 'lemon' and 'buff' have been avoided, the generic term 'yellow' being used throughout. Similarly, the term 'red' has been used to cover a wide variety of shades. It is also difficult to differentiate between a band and a ring, generally the latter term has only been used for a very thin dividing line.

The colours listed are those normally used by the owning company and it must be borne in mind that vessels may frequently be chartered to other operators and appear in the chartering company's livery. Where such an arrangement has some degree of permanence, the fact has been noted, e.g. in the case of the Irish Shelbourne Shipping Co. whose fleet works for the British & Irish Steam Packet Co. Conversely, ships flying the Dutch, German, or some other foreign flag may frequently be encountered in the colours of a British operator while on charter and this fact has also been noted where it is a regular practice.

Introduction

BRITISH COASTAL SHIPS, TUGS AND TRAWLERS is the successor to the popular Ian Allan ABC Books on coastal shipping first published in 1953. Whereas the earlier books dealt only with coastal passenger and cargo ships of over 200 gross tons, the present volume has been extended to cover fleet lists of some four hundred different companies operating coastal and short-sea passenger, cargo and container ships, coastal tankers, sand-carriers, tugs, trawlers, dredgers and oil-rig supply vessels, as well as pilot tenders and lighthouse supply ships. It is the author's hope that it will thus provide an almost complete survey of the smaller units which make up the British Mercantile Marine and which may be encountered in British ports or around the British Isles.

The book has been divided into the following sections with a single index to all the companies mentioned in each section:

Coastal and Near-Sea Passenger and Cargo Ships. Although generally restricted to those companies whose fleets trade in coastal waters or within Norway to Brest limits, the extension in the use of smaller units for the Mediterranean Trade and in connection with the ever-increasing container trades has meant that for the sake of completeness some fleets have been included which may well be found very much further afield. Others, with very much more restricted areas of activity, such as the sand and gravel dredgers and carriers, the effluent tankers, as well as some salvage craft, are included in this section.

Pilot, Lighthouse and Buoy Tenders. This section includes the vessels of Trinity House and other lighthouse and harbour authorities which operate craft of these types of over 200 gross tons.

Oil-Rig Servicing, Supply and Research Vessels, setting out full lists of all British flag vessels of this kind, including unavoidably some units which at a given time may be working on contract work in very distant areas.

The section on Dredgers and Other Harbour Craft has been restricted to self-propelled dredgers (with a note on the type of equipment installed) and the hopper barges used in conjunction with them. Space has precluded the listing of such other harbour units as floating cranes and suction elevators.

All Tugs of over 30 gross tons are believed to have been included, with the exception of some units which are at present laid-up and awaiting possible sale or breaking up and a few which are privately owned and do not now trade commercially. Some of the larger and more interesting tugs working on inland waters within the United Kingdom have been mentioned.

The final chapter lists all Trawlers and Drifter-Trawlers of over 100 gross tons. In some trawler fleet lists, difficulty has been experienced in keeping pace with the large number of changes which are currently taking place in the ownership or management of vessels by subsidiary companies within the major groups of trawler owners and the lists may not necessarily be completely up-to-date for this reason.

Inevitably in a book of this kind changes must take place between the preparation of the manuscript and the date of publication, and some errors and omissions will almost certainly occur. The author would like to apologise for these in advance and would be grateful for any help or suggestions which would make any future edition more complete.

Acknowledgements are due to the many Shipping Companies which have readily given information; to Lloyds Register; to the Central Record of the World Ship Society; the Port of Lowestoft Research Society; and to very many individuals, amongst whom Mervyn Gaston, David King, Gilbert Mayes, R.N., Charles Traill, Peter White and T. J. M. Wood. Without the help of all these the book would never have been possible. Thanks are also due to those many individual and companies who have supplied the photographs.

October 1971

D. RIDLEY CHESTERTON

The
WORLD SHIP SOCIETY

offers unrivalled facilities for a modest annual subscription.

Keep the fleet lists in Coastal Ships up to date by joining the World Ship Society.

These facilities include:

★   Illustrated magazine, MARINE NEWS monthly with world-wide news coverage and articles on all types of ships and shipping.

★   Branches, with regular meetings and visits to ports and ships.

★   Research media.

★   Postal contacts throughout the world.

Send 3p stamp for details and magazines:

WORLD SHIP SOCIETY, Dept. C.S.
HENGISTBURY, 431 GREEN LANE
COVENTRY, CV3 6EL.

COASTAL AND SHORT-SEA SHIPS

ABERDEEN COAL & SHIPPING CO. LTD.
Aberdeen

FUNNEL: *Black with white band between two red bands.* HULL: *Black with red boot-topping and white line.*

Name	Built	Tons	Length	Breadth	Speed	Engines
Ferryhill II	1971	199	137	25	9	M(A)

ALBRIGHT & WILSON, LTD.
Whitehaven

FUNNEL: *Blue with white "AW" monogram, or in colours of J. Fisher & Sons Ltd.* HULL: *Grey with red boot-topping.*

Marchon Enterprise	1962	1,599	261	39	12	M(A)
Marchon Venturer	1962	1,599	261	39	12	M(A)

See also J. Fisher & Sons, Ltd.

ALDERNEY SHIPPING CO. LTD.
Alderney, C.I.

FUNNEL: *Blue with black disc containing yellow letters "A S C".* HULL: *Black with red boot-topping.*

Alderney Courier*	1940	203	116	21	7½	M(A)
ex Reiger–70, Wilca–65, Rejo–56, Capricorn–55, Wim–54, Tasman						
Alderney Trader	1952	370	147	25	10½	M(A)
ex Glenbride–69, Lady Silvia–63						

*Owned by Link Services Ltd.

ALLANTONE SUPPLIES LTD.
(GASELEE & SON (FELIXSTOWE) LTD.)
Felixstowe

FUNNEL: *As Gaselee.* HULL: *Black with red boot-topping.*

Coastal Tankers:						
Contractor	1950	161	121	19	7	M(A)
ex Regent Wren–71						
Conveyor	—	—	—	—	—	M(A)
ex Broachdale H.–71						

ALLIED MILLS LTD.

FUNNEL:				HULL:					
Severn Side	...	...	...	1952	244	134	21	7½	M(A)

AMEY MARINE LTD.
Southampton

FUNNEL: *Blue with black letter "P" and yellow swallow-tail flag over black-edged white panel with the word "AMEY" in black on white band.* HULL: *Black or blue with red boot-topping.*

Sand Dredgers and Carriers:

Allard				1938	349	247	25	8	M(A)
ex Mallard–64, West Coaster–50									
Pen Arun				1943	311	141	21	8	M(A)
ex Lantyan–Roselyne									
Pen Avon				1966	787	200	34	10	M(A)
Pen Dart				1957	499	174	30	9	M(A)
ex Sand Dart–64									
Pen Stour				1970	1,582	264	46	11	M(A)
Pen Taw				1968	349	156	29	9	M(A)
Pen Yar				1955	693	180	37	8½	M(A)
ex Laga II–69									
Wm. Woolaway				1964	355	156	29	9	M(A)

ANTLER LTD.
London

FUNNEL:				HULL:					
Willmary				1966	200	137	25	8½	M(A)

E. B. APPLETON
Middlesbrough

FUNNEL: | HULL: *Black.*

Coastal Bunkering Tanker:

Cherrybobs				1950	257	—	—	9½	M(A)
ex Rosedale H.–70									

D. ARNOLD
Southampton

FUNNEL: *Grey with broad red band.* HULL: *Grey with red boot-topping.*

Sand Dredgers and Carriers:

Sand Robin				1950	116	91	19	7	M(A)
ex Regent Robin–67									
Sjona				1951	205	120	20	13	M(A)
ex Nesna–67									

10

F. A. ASHMEAD & SON, LTD.
Bristol

FUNNEL: *Black with red letter "A" on white band between two narrow red bands*
HULL: *Black or grey with red boot-topping.*

Beau Leigh	...	...	...	1937	122	96	18	8	M(A)

See also Tugs.

ASHMEAD (PADSTOW) LTD.
Padstow

FUNNEL: *Black with red letter "A" on white band between two narrow red bands.*
HULL: *Grey with red boot-topping.*

Sand Dredgers and Carriers:

Stowmead	...	...	...	1933	377	—	—	—	M(A)

ASSOCIATED HUMBER LINES LTD.
Hull

FUNNEL: *Yellow with black top and black letters "A H L" on broad red band.*
HULL: *Black or grey with red boot-topping.*

Humber Ferries: (Operated for British Railways Board)

Lincoln Castle	...	...	1940	598	209	56	10	SR(PW)
Tattershall Castle	...	...	1934	556	209	57	10	SR(PW)
Wingfield Castle ...	...	...	1934	556	209	57	10	SR(PW)

ATLANTIC STEAM NAVIGATION CO. LTD.
London

FUNNEL: *Blue with black top separated by broad white band.* HULL: *Black with white line and red boot-topping.*

Car and Vehicle Ferries:

Bardic Ferry	...	...	...	1957	2,550	339	55	14	M(2)
Celtic Ferry				1943	5,556	462	73	13½	ST(2)
ex German Navy LSD.WS.1–66, City of Havana–Jose Marti–H.M.S. Northway									
Europic Ferry	...	...	...	1968	4,190	451	69	19¼	M(2)
Gaelic Ferry	...	...	...	1964	2,756	366	56	16	M(2)

Ministry of Transport:

Cerdic Ferry	...	...	...	1961	2,563	361	55	14	M(2)
Doric Ferry	...	...	...	1962	2,573	361	55	14	M(2)
Ionic Ferry	...	...	...	1958	2,557	338	55	14	M(2)

The Company also employs chartered tonnage.

R. S. BANYARD (COLCHESTER SHIPPING CO.)
Colchester

FUNNEL: *Yellow with black top.* HULL: *Black.*

Mary Birch	1915	157	106	21	6½	M(Aux)
ex Swanage–35, ex Admiralty X-Lighter						
P. R. Banyard:						
Carita	1913	140	96	26	8	M(A)

BELCON SHIPPING & TRADING CO. LTD.
London

FUNNEL: HULL:

Croydon	1951	1,871	275	39	10½	M(A)
Sydenham	1951	1,871	275	39	10½	M(A)

BELFAST STEAMSHIP CO. LTD.
(COAST LINES GROUP)
Belfast

FUNNEL: *Red with black top.* HULL: *Black with white line and red boot-topping.*

Car and Vehicle Ferries:						
Ulster Prince	1967	4,270	377	54	17½	M(2)
Ulster Queen	1967	4,270	377	54	17½	M(2)

L. G. BEVAN (SOUTH WALES SAND & GRAVEL CO. LTD.)
Swansea

FUNNEL: HULL:

Sand Dredgers and Carriers:						
Glen Gower	1963	552	169	30	10	M(A)
Glen Hafod	1960	552	169	30	10	M(A)

G. V. BLAKE
London

FUNNEL: *Red with black top.* HULL: *Black with red boot-topping.*

Frederick Hughes	1956	311	135	25	8½	M(A)
ex Berwyn Baron–66, Grouville–64, Errol–58, Kestor–39						

BOWKER & KING, LTD.
London

FUNNEL: *Black with houseflag (Quartered diagonally white over blue over white, with white diamond bearing the blue letters "B K" superimposed). On white upperworks where no funnel.* HULL: *Black.*

Thames or Bristol Channel Tankers:

Babingdon	1952	446	168	34	8½	M(A)
ex Esso Abingdon–66						
Baccarat ...	1959	293	150	29	8½	M(A)
Batsman ...	1963	217	115	25	8½	M(A)
Beaufort ...	1963	347	150	29	8	M(A)
ex Beefeater–69						
Beechcroft ...	1966	556	159	34	9½	M(A)
Beresford ...	1959	304	138	27	7½	M(A)
Berkeley ...	1969	730	212	30	10	M(A)
Bisley ...	1969	700	211	30	10	M(A)
Black Knight ...	1960	481	169	34	10	M(A)
Blackfriars ...	1955	425	158	30	8½	M(A)
ex Mobilfuel–70						
Blakeley ...	1972	729	—	—	—	M(A)
Bold Knight ...	1960	464	170	34	9½	M(A)
Borman ...	1970	730	212	30	10	M(A)
Bouncer ...	1968	220	116	25	10	M(A)
Bowler ...	1963	217	115	25	8½	M(A)
Bridgeness ...	1969	797	187	36	10	M(A)
Bristolian ...	1969	797	187	36	10	M(A)
Bude ...	1972	730	—	—	—	M(A)
Budleigh ...	1969	550	159	34	9½	M(A)
ex John T. Stratford–69						
Burgundy ...	1962	323	135	29	10	M(A)
Busby	1963	200	115	25	10	M(A)

R. S. BRIGGS & CO. (SHIPPING) LTD.
London

FUNNEL: *Black with house flag on broad blue band between two narrow white bands* HULL: *Black with red boot-topping.*

Katie H. ...	1952	635	200	30	10½	M(A)
ex Earlsfield–69, Coquetdyke–56						

Brigdale Shipping Ltd:

Ethel B. ...	1953	1,231	229	35	11½	M(A)
ex Harfry–69, Tana–63						

BRISTOL STEAM NAVIGATION CO. LTD.
Bristol

FUNNEL: *Yellow with houseflag (White with red St Andrew's Cross and blue letters "B S N C" in each quarter.* HULL: *Black with white line and red boot-topping.*

Apollo ...	1954	1,254	278	39	10½	M(A)
Echo ...	1957	1,241	278	40	12¼	M(A)

Bowker & King Ltd.   M.V. BORMAN

BRITISH DREDGING (SHIPPING) LTD.
London, Bristol & Cardiff

FUNNEL: *Red with black top.* HULL: *Black with red boot-topping.*

Sand Dredgers and Carriers:

Badminton	1956	610	154	33	9½	M(A)
Bowbelle	1964	1,486	262	45	11¾	M(A)
Bowcrest	1955	587	179	30	9½	M(A)
Bowcross	1967	940	196	39	10	M(A)
ex Chichester Cross—71						
Bowfleet	1965	1,620	265	45	11½	M(A)
Bowline	1953	596	179	29	9½	M(A)
Bowprince	1964	1,599	264	45	11½	M(A)
Bowqueen	1963	1,317	258	40	12½	M(A)
Bowsprite	1967	1,503	264	46	12½	M(A)
Bowstar	1950	561	169	28	9½	M(A)
Bowtrader	1969	1,592	283	48	12	M(A)
Camerton	1950	891	176	33	9½	M(A)

Bristol Sand & Gravel Co.

Peterston	1961	748	176	33	11	M(A)

BRITISH RAILWAYS BOARD
(Shipping & International Services Divn.)
and other companies operating as
SEALINK

FUNNEL: *Red with black top and British Rail "Twin-Arrow" device, except as follow: S.N.C.F: Yellow with black top (with addition of ex LBSC houseflag on Newhaven–Dieppe vessels); Belgian Marine: Yellow with black top separated by red over white over blue bands; A.L.A: "ALA" monogram instead of "Twin-Arrow".* HULL: *Dark blue or black with red boot-topping, with or without white line.*

Passenger Ships:

Avalon	1963	6,707	404	60	21	ST(2)
Caesarea	1960	3,992	322	54	18½	ST(2)
Cambria	1949	5,284	397	56	15	M(2)
Dover	1965	3,602	369	57	19½	ST(2)
Duke of Argyll	1956	4,450	376	57	21	ST(2)
Duke of Lancaster	1956	4,797	376	57	21	ST(2)
Duke of Rothesay	1956	4,780	376	57	21	ST(2)
Falaise	1947	2,416	311	50	15	ST(2)
Hengist	1972	—	—	—	—	M(2)
Hibernia	1949	5,284	397	56	15	M(2)
Holyhead Ferry I	1965	3,879	369	57	19½	ST(2)
Horsa	1972	—	—	—	—	M(2)
Lord Warden	1952	3,333	362	61	14	ST(2)
Maid of Kent	1959	3,920	373	60	14	ST(2)
Maid of Orleans	1949	3,777	341	52	15	ST(2)
Normannia	1952	2,219	309	50	14	ST(2)
Sarnia	1961	3,989	322	53	19½	ST(2)
St George	1968	7,356	420	68	21	M(2)

British Transport Ship Management (Scotland) Ltd.

Ailsa Princess	1971	3,960	369	57	20½	M(2)
Antrim Princess	1967	3,630	369	57	19½	M(2)
Caledonian Princess	1961	3,630	353	57	19	ST(2)
Dalriada*	1971	—	—	—	—	M

Belgian State Marine (Belgian flag)

Artevelde ...	1958	2,812	383	52	21	M(2)
Koning Albert	1948	3,701	373	49	22	M(2)
Koningen Elisabeth	1957	3,795	374	50	22	M(2)
Koningen Fabiola	1962	3,057	385	52	20	M(2)
Prince Philippe ...	1948	3,701	372	49	22	M(2)
Prinses Josephine-Charlotte ...	1949	2,572	375	49	20	M(2)
Prinses Paola	1966	4,356	384	52	24	M(2)
Reine Astrid	1958	3,795	374	50	22	M(2)
Roi Baudouin	1965	3,241	387	52	21	M(2)
Roi Leopold III	1956	3,794	374	50	22	M(2)

Soc. Nat. des Chemins de Fer Francais (French flag):

Chantilly	1965	3,400	361	58	20	M(2)
Compiegne	1958	3,467	377	60	20	M(2)
Cote d'Azur	1951	3,998	365	51	21½	ST(2)
Valencay	1965	3,477	344	56	21	M(2)
Villandry	1964	3,445	344	58	21	M(2)

Stoomvaart Maats. 'Zeeland' (Netherlands flag):

Koningen Juliana	1968	6,682	430	67	21	M(2)
Koningin Wilhelmina	1960	6,228	394	57	21	M(2)

Train Ferries:

Cambridge Ferry	1963	3,294	403	61	13½	M(2)
Essex Ferry	1957	3,089	400	61	12½	M(2)
Norfolk Ferry	1951	3,157	400	61	12½	M(2)
Shepperton Ferry	1935	2,996	360	63	12½	ST(2)
Suffolk Ferry	1947	3,134	404	61	12½	M(2)
Vortigern	1969	4,371	377	63	19½	M(2)

S.A. de Nav. Angleterre–Lorraine–Alsace (French flag)

Twickenham Ferry ...	1934	2,839	360	61	16½	ST(2)

Soc. Nat. des Chemins de Fer Francais (French flag)

Saint-Germain	1951	3,094	380	61	16½	M(2)

Cargo Ships:

Brian Boroime	1971	—	352	57	14	M(2A)
Colchester	1959	1,946	296	38	13	M(A)
Container Enterprise	1958	1,000	263	42	10	M(A)
Container Venturer	1958	1,000	263	42	10	M(A)
Elk	1959	795	228	40	14	M(A)
Harrogate	1959	871	232	39	12½	M(A)
Isle of Ely	1958	1,946	296	38	13	M(A)
Moose	1959	795	228	40	12	M(A)
Rhodri Mawr	1971	4,095	352	57	14	M(2A)
Sea Freightliner I ...	1967	4,034	389	55	13½	M(2A)
Sea Freightliner II	1968	4,100	388	55	13½	M(2A)
Selby	1959	963	232	39	12½	M(A)
Slieve Bawn	1937	1,573	310	47	12	ST(2)
Slieve Bearnagh	1936	1,485	310	47	12	ST(2)
Slieve Donard	1960	1,569	310	47	13½	M(2)

Belgian State Marine (Belgian flag)

Ijzer	1953	1,171	219	40	15	M

Soc. Nat. des Chemins de Fer Francais (French flag)

Transcontainer I	1968	2,760	341	61	16	M(2A)

Isle of Wight Ferries:

Brading	1948	837	200	48	12	M(2)
Camber Queen	1961	293	166	43	10½	M(2)
Cuthred	1969	704	190	52	10½	M(2)
Farringford	1947	489	178	50	10½	ME(PW)
Fishbourne	1961	293	166	43	10½	M(2)
Freshwater	1959	363	164	42	10½	M(2)
Lymington	1938	275	148	37	9	M
Shanklin	1951	833	200	48	14½	M(2)
Southsea	1948	837	200	48	12	M(2)

See also Associated Humber Lines Ltd. and Caledonian Steam Packet Co. Ltd.

British Rail M.V. CUTHRED

[*John G. Callis*]

British Rail   M.V. ISLE OF ELY

British Rail   M.V. ANTRIM PRINCESS

BRITISH ROAD SERVICES LTD.
Newport, I.O.W.

FUNNEL: *Yellow with black top separated by narrow green band.* HULL: *Black with green topline and "BRITISH ROAD SERVICES" in white.*

Covert	1950	133	81	20	8	M(2A)
Crop	1950	133	81	20	8	M(2A)
Mount	1938	118	76	19	6	M(2A)
Northwood	1962	171	100	23	8½	M(2A)

BROOKBANK SHIPPING CO. LTD.
London

FUNNEL: *Red with two interlocking blue letters "BB" on broad white band.* HULL: *Black with yellow line and red boot-topping.*

Brookbank Trader	1953	429	161	25	11	M(A)
ex Meuse–70						

M. J. BROWN
Kings Lynn

FUNNEL: HULL:

Citadel	1950	369	138	25	9	M(A)

T. R. BROWN & SONS
(HOLMS SAND & GRAVEL CO. LTD.)
Bristol & Greenock

FUNNEL: *Black with broad red band between two narrow white bands.* HULL: *Black with red boot-topping.*

Sand Dredgers and Carriers:						
Colonsay	1945	146	—	—	7	SR(A)
Harry Brown	1962	634	172	33	10½	M(A)
Norleader	1967	1,600	240	44	12	M(A)
Portway	1927	298	122	24	9	SR(A)

A. J. BRUSH, LTD.
Maldon

FUNNEL: HULL:

Sand Dredgers and Carriers:						
Doddles	1915	121	96	20	7	M(A)
ex Admiralty X-Lighter						
Purbeck	1936	199	103	24	8¾	M(A)

BURIES MARKES, LTD.
London

FUNNEL: *Black with blue letters "B M" on broad white band between two narrow red bands.* HULL: *Black with white line and white boot-topping.*

Chemical Tankers:

La Hacienda	...	...	...	1969	1,452	264	42	13	M(A)
La Quinta	...	...	...	1969	1,452	264	42	13½	M(A)
(New)	...	...	...	1972	—	—	—	—	M(A)

BURNS & LAIRD LINES, LTD.
(COAST LINES GROUP)
Glasgow

FUNNEL: *Red with black top separated by narrow blue band.* HULL: *Black with white line and red boot-topping.*

Lairdsfox	...	...	...	1952	562	189	31	10	M(A)
ex Foxfield–66, Leemans–54								
Lairdsglen	...	...	...	1954	1,496	298	43	14	M(2)
Car and Vehicle Ferry:								
Lion	...	...	...	1967	3,333	365	56	20½	M(2)

BURRY SAND CO. LTD.
Llanelly

FUNNEL: HULL: *Black.*

Sand Dredgers and Carriers:

Coedmor	...	...	...	1946	181	108	20	9	M(A)
ex Arran Monarch–64, Vic 57–48								
Orselina	...	...	...	1938	249	136	24	9½	M(A)
ex Ebbrix–60, Brixham–40								

CAINES & BOWEN
Southampton

FUNNEL: *Black with narrow white over red over narrow white bands over broad red bands.* HULL: *Black or grey with red boot-topping.*

Sand Dredgers and Carriers:

Baymead	...	1944	330	152	24	8	M(A)
ex Chartsman–66, Empire Boxer–46							
Ben Olliver	...	1935	137	90	19	8	M(A)
Lady Sonia	...	1929	108	—	21	7	M(A)
ex Parkstone–54, Apollinaris III–37							
Mark Bowen	...	—	—	—	—	—	M(A)
ex Chattenden–67							

CALEDONIAN STEAM PACKET CO. LTD.
(SCOTTISH TRANSPORT GROUP)
Glasgow

FUNNEL: *Yellow with black top and red Scottish lion device.* HULL: *Dark blue with red boot-topping.*

Countess of Breadalbane	...	1936	106	95	19	10	M(2)
Duchess of Hamilton	... ...	1932	801	272	35	16	ST(3)
Maid of Argyll ...	... ...	1953	508	165	30	14	M(2)
Maid of Ashton ...	... ...	1953	508	165	30	14	M(2)
Maid of Cumbrae		1953	508	165	30	14	M(2)
Maid of Skelmorlie *ALA (GK)*		1953	508	165	30	14	M(2)
Queen Mary II	... ...	1933	1,013	263	35	19	ST(3)
Car and Vehicle Ferries:							
Caledonia	...	1966	1,156	203	41	15	M(2)
ex Stena Baltica–69							
Arran	...	1953	568	186	36	15	M(2)
Bute	...	1954	568	186	36	15	M(2)
Cowall	...	1954	569	186	36	15	M(2)
Glen Sannox	...	1957	1,107	257	46	17	M(2)
Kyleakin	...	1970	225	161	42	8	M(2)
Loch Lomond Service:							
Maid of the Loch ...	...	1953	555	208	51	12	SR(PW)

Also smaller ferries of under 100 g.r.t. See also British Railways Board (British Transport Ship Management (Scotland) Ltd).

Caledonian Steam Packet Co.   M.V. COWALL   [*William J. Harris*

CAMBRIDGE (TANKERS) LTD.
(DUNDEE, PERTH & LONDON SHIPPING CO. LTD.)
London

FUNNEL: *Red with black top.* HULL: *Black with red boot-topping.*

Coastal Tankers:						
Kingennie	1958	1,169	232	37	11	M(A)

CARDIGAN SHIPPING CO. LTD.
(BLANDFORD SHPG. CO. LTD.)
London

FUNNEL: HULL:

Bravo Contender	1968	1,204	301	59	15	M(A)
ex Sealord Contender–69						

JOSEPH CARNEY & SONS LTD.
Sunderland

FUNNEL: *Black with white over red bands.* HULL: *Black with red boot-topping.*

Ash Hopper Barges:						
Cairnside	1927	591	176	36	9	SR(A)
ex G–64						
Millside	1921	592	175	32	9	SR(A)
ex T.I.C. No 18–65						
Simonside	1931	671	—	—	9½	SR(A)

CENTRAL ELECTRICITY GENERATING BOARD
London

FUNNEL: *Red with black top and black rings.* HULL: *Black with white topline and red boot-topping.*

Barford	1950	3,357	339	46	10½	SR(A)
Captain J. M. Donaldson ...	1951	3,341	339	46	10½	SR(A)
Charles H. Merz	1955	2,947	340	43	11½	SR(A)
Cliff Quay	1950	3,345	339	46	10½	SR(A)
James Rowan	1955	2,947	340	44	11¼	SR(A)
Lord Citrine	1950	3,357	339	46	10½	SR(A)
Sir Archibald Page ...	1950	3,345	339	46	10½	SR(A)
Sir John Snell	1955	2,947	340	47	11	SR(A)
Sir Johnstone Wright ...	1955	3,382	339	47	11	SR(A)
Sir William Walker ...	1954	2,901	340	44	11¼	SR(A)
W. J. H. Wood	1951	3,345	339	46	10½	SR(A)

Thames "Up-River" or "Flatiron" Colliers:

Battersea	1951	1,777	271	40	11	M(A)
Blackwall Point	1951	1,776	271	40	11	M(A)
Brimsdown	1951	1,837	271	40	10	SR(A)
Brunswick Wharf	1951	1,782	271	40	10½	SR(A)
Dame Caroline Haslett	1950	1,777	271	40	11	M(A)
Deptford	1951	1,782	271	40	10½	SR(A)
Hackney	1952	1,782	271	40	10½	SR(A)
Harry Richardson	1950	1,777	271	40	11	M(A)

Hopper Barges:

Bessie Surtees	1955	561	158	33	10¾	M(A)
Sir Fon	1950	814	185	36	11¼	M(A)

Central Electricity Generating Board   M.V. CAPTAIN J. M. DONALDSON
[*John G. Callis*

CHARRINGTON, GARDNER, LOCKET (LONDON) LTD.
London

FUNNEL: *Yellow with black top and broad blue band between two narrow white bands.* HULL: *Black with red boot-topping.*

Thames Tankers:

Charcrest	1964	465	163	34	8¾	M(A)
Charmo	1960	477	163	34	10	M(A)

CHESHAM SHIPPING CO. LTD.
London

FUNNEL: *As Briggs.* HULL: *Blue with red boot-topping.*

Francis B. ... ... ex *Blisworth–71*	1957	1,031	213	31	10½	M(A)
Valerie B. ... ... ex *Sarsfield–70, Edgefield–65, Spolesto–56*	1956	622	203	34	10½	M(A)

Civil & Marine Ltd.   M.V. CAMBROOK   [*A. Duncan*

CIVIL & MARINE, LTD.
London

FUNNEL: *Red with black top separated by narrow white and white letters "C M".* HULL: *Black with red boot-topping.*

Beverley Brook	1941	245	130	25	8	M(A)
Wall Brook	1940	244	130	25	8	M(A)
Sand Dredgers and Carriers:						
Cambrook	1967	1,574	250	54	11½	M(A)
Peterna	1915	154	105	21	—	M(A)
ex Helen Birch–51, Studland, Admiralty- ex Lighter						

COAST LINES LTD.
(P. & O. GROUP)
Liverpool

FUNNEL: *Black with white chevron. (Vessels may also operate in the colours of Link Line Ltd. or other associated companies).* HULL: *Black with black boot-topping separated by broad white band.*

Lancashire Coast	1954	1,020	256	39	12	M(A)
ex Trojan Prince–69, Lancashire Coast–68						
Pointer	1956	1,208	224	37	11½	M(A)
ex Birchfield–59						
Spaniel	1955	1,207	224	37	11½	M(A)
ex Brentfield –59						
Terrier	1957	1,127	220	35	11½	M(A)
ex Stege–63, Emma Robert–59						
Wirral Coast	1962	881	203	36	12	M(A)

See also Belfast S.S.Co., Burns & Laird Lines Ltd., North of Scotland & Orkney S.N. Co., and Tyne-Tees Steam Shpg. Co.

S. W. COE & CO. LTD.
Liverpool

FUNNEL: *Yellow with black top separated by white over red bands.* HULL: *Grey or black with red boot-topping.*

Blackthorn	1960	749	190	34	11	M(A)
Maythorn	1962	771	190	35	11	M(A)
Redthorn	1962	472	191	30	11	M(A)
ex Oranmore–70						
Thorn Line Finance Ltd:						
Firethorn	1967	1,051	220	38	12	M(A)
Hawthorn	1952	1,054	217	35	11	M(A)
ex Harglen–68, Irish Heather–64						
Whitethorn	1963	1,589	261	40	14	M(A)
ex Hero –70						

COLCHESTER SHIPPING CO. LTD.
See R. S. Banyard

COMMODORE SHIPPING CO. LTD.
Guernsey, C.I.

FUNNEL: *Blue with golden lion device.* HULL: *Dark blue with white line and red boot-topping.*

Commodore Goodwill ...	1958	499	196	33	12½	M(A)
ex *Goodwill–68*						
Commodore Trader	1971	460	—	—	—	(MA)
Channel Transporters (Portsmouth) Ltd:						
Island Commodore	1971	499	226	36	12	M(A)
Norman Commodore	1970	299	226	36	12	M(A)

D. COOK, LTD.
Hull

FUNNEL: *Red with black top.* HULL: *Black.*

Humber Tankers:						
Onward Pioneer	1955	164	122	19	8	M(A)
S. T. Morgan	1915	139	106	21	7	M(A)
ex *Admiralty X-Lighter*						

Also smaller vessels of under 100 g.r.t.

W. COOPER & SONS, LTD.
Widnes

FUNNEL: *Yellow with black top.* HULL: *Grey with black boot-topping.*

Sand Dredgers and Carriers:						
William Cooper	1965	553	157	34	9½	M(A)

D. COPESTAKE
London

FUNNEL: *Black with red over black over red bands.* HULL: *Black with grey topsides.*

Hoocreek	1928	209	117	21	7	M(A)
ex *Herb–62, Rhone–60, Seine–35*						

CORNISH SHIPPING LTD.
(HARRIS & CO. (SHIPPING) LTD.)
Par

FUNNEL:		HULL:					
Vauban	1962	370	148	23	10	M(A)

CORONET SHIPPING CO. LTD.
London

FUNNEL:		HULL:					
Narya	1971	1,600	278	42	—	M(A)
Nenya	1971	1,600	278	42	—	M(A)
Vilya	1971	1,600	278	42	—	M(A)

CORY MARITIME LTD.
London

FUNNEL: *Black with black diamond on broad white band.* HULL: *Black with red boot-topping.*

Liquid Gas Tankers Ltd:						
Corbank	1956	2,334	305	40	12	M(A)
Corbeach	1957	2,106	277	40	12	M(A)
Corburn ...	1953	2,059	279	39	10	M(A)
Corchester	1965	4,840	370	53	12	M(A)
Corsea *KAPPA PROGRESS (CY)*	1957	3,373	339	46	10	M(A)
Corstar *KAPPA ENTERPRISE (CY)*	1956	3,379	339	46	10	M(A)
Corstream	1955	3,330	339	46	9½	M(A)
Coastal Tankers:						
Cordale*	1970	784	201	32	12¼	M(A)
Cordene*	1970	784	201	32	12¼	M(A)
Pass of Dalveen ...	1958	965	217	32	11½	M(A)
Pass of Glenclunie ...	1963	1,416	245	38	11½	M(A)
Pass of Glenogle ...	1963	860	203	33	11½	M(A)
Pass of Melfort	1961	937	215	34	11½	M(A)

See also Cory Tank Craft Ltd., and Cory Lighterage Ltd., Cory Ship Towage Ltd., and Cory Ship Towage (Clyde) Ltd. in Tug Section.
*Liquid Gas Carriers.

CORY TANK CRAFT LTD.
London

FUNNEL: *Black with black diamond on broad white band.* HULL: *Black with red boot-topping.*

Thames Tankers:						
Battle Stone	1968	293	—	—	8	M(A)
Bruce Stone	1964	357	143	30	11	M(A)
Druid Stone	1967	236	119	26	7½	M(A)
London Stone	1957	438	155	31	11	M(A)
Rebus Stone	1963	177	—	—	—	M(A)
Rufus Stone	1963	165	—	—	—	M(A)
Wade Stone	1968	180	—	—	7½	M(A)

Commodore Shipping Co. M.V. COMMODORE GOODWILL [*John G. Callis*

Cory Maritime Ltd. M.V. PASS OF DALVEEN [*R. J. Weeks*

COX & WILTSHIRE, LTD.
London

FUNNEL: HULL: *Grey.*

Catherina W.	1949	250	141	22	8½	M(A)
ex *Meeuw–55*						

HUGH CRAIG & CO. LTD.
(CAWOOD HOLDINGS LIMITED)
Belfast

FUNNEL: *Yellow with black top and Cawood Wharton monogram in black inside black circle.* HULL: *Black with red boot-topping.*

Craigmore	1965	1,359	240	37	11	M(A)

CROSON, LTD.
Poole

FUNNEL: HULL:

Bournemouth area Excursion Vessels:						
Bournemouth Queen	1935	227	130	26	10	M(2)
ex *Coronia–68*						
Poole Queen	1941	127	—	—	—	M(2)
ex *Matapan–68*						
Wessex Queen	1962	121	—	—	—	M(2)
ex *Swanage Belle–68*						

W. G. S. CROUCH & SONS, LTD.
Greenhithe

FUNNEL: HULL:

Ernie Spearing	1945	138	104	20	8	M(A)
ex *Attunity–67*						
Harriet Spearing	1924	115	90	19	7½	M(A)
ex *Stourgate–63*						
William Spearing	1945	136	100	20	8	M(A)
ex *Apexity–65*						
Coastal Tanker-:						
British Maiden	1924	102	—	—	—	M(A)

D. CUMMING & CO. LTD.
(FIFE SHIPPING CO. LTD.)
London

FUNNEL: *Yellow.*   HULL: *Green with brown boot-topping.*

Joan C.	1957	526	185	29	10	M(A)
ex Antilla–70						

R. CUNNINGHAM (SCALPAY) CO. LTD.
(R. CAMERON & CO. LTD.)
Stornaway

FUNNEL: *Yellow with black top and white over blue over red bands.*   HULL: *Grey with black boot-topping.*

Isle of Harris	1940	274	142	23	10	M(A)
ex Floro–65, Maria S: –62						
Eilean Glas	1961	374	156	25	10	M(A)
ex Ceres–71, Overysel–68						

Also the wooden m.v. Isle of Canna and Isle of Skye, both under 100 g.r.t.

CURRIE LINE LTD.
(WALTER RUNCIMAN & CO. LTD.)
Leith

FUNNEL: *Black with broad white band.*   HULL: *Black with red boot-topping and the words "CURRIE LINE" in white letters amidships.*

Pentland	1958	821	225	36	11	M(A)
Zealand	1955	2,238	318	45	12½	M

A. S. DAVIDSON, LTD.
(CAWOOD HOLDINGS LTD.)
Belfast

FUNNEL: *Red with black top separated by broad yellow and narrow blue band.*
HULL: *Black with red boot-topping.*

Mayfair Sapphire	1949	1,032	214	34	10½	M(A)
ex Sapphire–58						

J. & A. DAVIDSON, LTD.
Aberdeen

FUNNEL: *Black with white letter "D" superimposed on green over red bands.*
HULL: *Black.*

Torquay	1963	443	167	27	11		M(A)
ex Roscrea–64							

ONESIMUS DOREY & SONS, LTD.
Guernsey, C.I.

FUNNEL: *Black with blue letter "D" on white diamond on red square interrupting blue band.* HULL: *Black with red boot-topping.*

Havelet	1964	1,042	217	34	11½	M(A)
Portelet	1961	1,052	217	34	11¼	M(A)

W. E. DOWDS, LTD.
Newport, Mon.

FUNNEL: *Green with black top.* HULL: *Black with red boot-topping.*

Brandon	1957	586	170	29	9	M(A)
Colston	1955	586	179	29	9	M(A)
Lorraine D.	1957	560	187	30	10	M(A)
ex Cambrian Coast–71						

G. DUPENOIS
Torquay

FUNNEL: *Black with three red bands interrupted by white "GD" monogram.*
HULL: *Black with red boot-topping.*

Friars Craig	1938	590	170	29	9	M(A)
ex Salcombe–69, Camroux IV–42						

EARNBANK SAND & GRAVEL CO. LTD.
(D. & R. TAYLOR, LTD.)
Perth

FUNNEL: *Blue with broad silver band.* HULL: *Black.*

Sand Dredgers and Carriers:						
Severn Merchant	1936	122	92	19	7½	M(A)
(Unnamed)	1933	311	129	25	9	M(A)
ex Antiquity–66						

EDDYSTONE SHIPPING CO. LTD.
(R. LAPTHORN & CO. LTD.)
Hoo, Kent

FUNNEL: *Red with black band with yellow star superimposed.* HULL: *Black with red boot-topping.*

Edward Stone	1965	196	109	22	8	M(A)

EFFLUENT SERVICES LTD.
Liverpool

FUNNEL: HULL: *Black with red boot-topping.*

Coastal Effluent Tanker:

Kinder	1944	465	159	26	9	M(A)
ex Anthony M.–70, Empire Tigity–47, Göhren–45						

EGGAR, FORRESTER (HOLDINGS) LTD.
London

FUNNEL: *Pale blue with dark blue stag head device.* HULL: *Grey with red boot-topping.*

Wib	1970	199	137	25	9	M(A)
Wiggs	1970	199	137	25	9	M(A)
Wilks	1969	199	137	25	9	M(A)
Wis	1970	199	137	25	9	M(A)
Wopper	1968	260	137	25	9½	M(A)
ex Continent–70						

ELDER DEMPSTER LINES LTD.
(OCEAN S.S. CO. LTD.)
Liverpool

FUNNEL: *Yellow.* HULL: *Black with red boot-topping.*

Car Carriers:

Carway JOLLYVERDE (IT)73	1967	866	296	49	14	M(A)
Clearway	1970	1,160	300	55	15	M(A)
ex Speedway–70						
Skyway	1963	1,175	302	57	15	M(2A)
ex Mandeville–70						
Speedway	1967	1,204	302	57	15	M(A)
ex Clearway–70, Sealord Challenger–69						

Vessels managed by the Mountwood Shipping Co Ltd.

ELLERMAN'S WILSON LINE, LTD.
Hull

FUNNEL: *Red with black top.*   HULL: *Dark green with red boot-topping, or grey with red boot-topping.*

Aaro	1960	2,468	330	49	13½	M
Destro ...	1970	1,571	360	63	17	M(2A)
Salerno *CITY OF CORINTH*	1965	1,559	308	46	13	M(A)
Salmo *CITY OF ATHENS*	1967	1,523	308	46	13	M(A)
Sangro *CITY OF ANKARA*	1968	1,523	308	46	13	M(A)
Silvio *CITY OF PATRAS*	1967	1,523	308	46	13	M(A)
Sorrento *CITY OF SPARTA* ...	1967	1,525	308	46	13	M(A)
Car and Vehicle Ferry:						
Spero *SAPPHO (GK)* ...	1966	6,916	454	68	18	M(2)
Svea Line (U.K.) Ltd. (Ellerman's Wilson—Mgrs)						
Garda	1965	1,598	308	45	13½	M(A)
ex Gudur–69						

ELLIS & McHARDY, LTD.
Aberdeen

FUNNEL: *Yellow with black top separated by red over black bands.*   HULL: *Black with red boot-topping.*

Spray	1962	890	195	33	11¼	M(A)

ELWICK BAY SHIPPING CO. LTD.
Stromness

FUNNEL: *Pale blue.*   HULL: *Black with red boot-topping (Carries crane amidships).*

Elwick Bay	1930	262	122	23	9	M(A)
ex Torwood–59, Plympton–48, Dartmeet–47, Norrix–46, Ellen M.–36						

ESKGARTH SHIPPING CO. LTD.
(COMBEN LONGSTAFF & CO. LTD.)
London

FUNNEL: *Black with white letters "ESK".* HULL: *Black with red boot-topping.*

Chevychase	1956	904	234	36	13	M(A)
Osborne Queen	1957	1,424	240	36	11½	M(A)
Eskglen Shipping Co. Ltd:						
Richmond Queen	1958	1,326	235	36	12	M(A)
ex Somerset Coast–59						
Sandringham Queen	1955	1,308	233	36	11	M(A)

Esso Petroleum Co.   M.V. ESSO LYNDHURST

[David W. Jenkins

ESSO PETROLEUM CO. LTD.
London

FUNNEL: *Black with red "Esso" device in blue ring on broad blue band.*   HULL: *Black or grey with red boot-topping.*

Coastal Tankers:

Esso Brixham	1957	758	196	34	10	M(A)
Esso Caernarvon	1962	1,103	231	36	10	M(A)
Esso Dover	1961	490	176	27	10	M(A)
Esso Fawley**	1967	11,046	534	72	16¾	M(A)
Esso Hythe	1959	856	209	35	10	M(A)
Esso Inverness	1971	2,200	300	42	13	M(A)
Esso Ipswich	1960	1,103	231	36	9½	M(A)
Esso Jersey	1961	313	123	24	9	M(A)
Esso Lyndhurst	1958	856	209	35	10	M(A)
Esso Milford Haven**	1968	11,046	354	72	16¾	M(A)
Esso Penzance	1971	2,169	300	42	13	M(A)
Esso Preston*	1956	1,965	299	42	10½	SR(A)
Esso Purfleet	1967	2,838	324	47	12	M(A)
Esso Tenby	1971	2,209	300	42	13¼	M(A)
Esso Tynemouth	1960	501	171	29	9½	M(A)
Esso Woolston	1958	856	210	35	10	M(A)

*Bitumen Tanker.   **Esso Fawley and Esso Milford Haven were built for coastal use.

F. T. EVERARD & SONS, LTD.
London

FUNNEL: *Black, or grey, or yellow, with red and white diagonally quartered houseflag.*   HULL: *Black with white topline and red boot-topping; Yellow with red or green boot-topping and the name "EVERARD" in large red letters amidships; or blue-grey or grey with red or black boot-topping.*

Ability	1943	881	203	30	10	M(A)
Actuality	1966	698	224	35	11	M(A)
Apricity	1967	692	224	35	11	M(A)
Centricity	1955	655	191	28	10	M(A)
Century	1956	770	204	30	10	M(A)
Continuity	1955	655	191	28	10	M(A)
Ethel Everard	1966	1,599	279	41	10	M(A)
Festivity	1963	199	110	25	8	M(A)
Fixity	1966	2,200	117	25	9	M(A)
Formality	1968	200	117	25	9	M(A)
Frederick T. Everard	1954	2,488	306	42	10	M(A)
Frivolity	1963	199	110	25	8	M(A)
Futurity	1968	198	110	25	9	M(A)
Georgina V. Everard	1955	2,487	306	42	10	M(A)
Penelope Everard	1963	1,583	265	39	11	M(A)
Rosemary Everard	1965	1,599	266	39	11	M(A)
Sagacity	1946	943	211	31	10	M(A)
Sanguity	1956	1,543	241	38	10½	M(A)
Scarcity	1948	584	177	28	10½	M(A)
Security	1971	1,599	279	42	11	M(A)
Selectivity	1952	1,575	241	38	10½	M(A)
Serenity	1970	1,590	279	42	11	M(A)
Severity	1954	590	184	28	10	M(A)
Similarity	1951	1,575	241	28	10½	M(A)
Sincerity	1971	1,599	279	42	11	M(A)
Sociality	1953	500	187	29	10	M(A)
ex June B.–53						
Sonority	1952	589	184	28	11	M(A)
Speciality	1951	1,539	241	38	10½	M(A)
William J. Everard	1963	1,589	266	39	10½	M(A)

✗ FRED EVERARD

F. T. EVERARD & SONS, LTD. *continued*

Coastal Tankers:

Acclivity	1968	299	168	28	10	M(A)
Activity	1969	698	243	34	11	M(A)
Agility	1959	1,016	214	35	11	M(A)
Alacrity	1966	943	216	35	12	M(A)
Allurity	1969	698	243	34	11	M(A)
Annuity	1961	1,600	266	40	10	M(A)
Aptity	1939	434	167	25	9	M(A)
Asperity	1967	698	236	32	12	M(A)
Assiduity	1964	1,249	234	36	11	M(A)
Audacity	1968	699	238	36	12	M(A)
Auspicity	1944	402	142	27	8	M(A)
ex Frans–55, Camagre–47, Chant 27–47						
Authority	1966	500	215	33	12	M(A)
Averity	1944	401	148	27	8	M(A)
ex Theodora–54, Chant 53–46						
Conformity	1940	484	172	28	9	SR(A)
ex C.85						
Totality	1945	149	100	20	7	SR(A)

Everard Shipping Co. Ltd.

Alignity	1945	890	201	32	9½	M(A)
ex Empire Fitzroy–52 ...						
Capacity	1963	461	170	28	9	M(A)
Clarity	1957	764	204	30	10	M(A)

Clydesdale Shipowners Ltd:

Gillian Everard	1963	1,598	266	39	11	M(A)
Grit	1966	498	220	34	12½	M(A)
ex Dagmar Stenhoj–70						

Scottish Navigation Co. Ltd.

Stability	1949	1,490	242	36	11	M(A)
Supremity	1970	698	265	45	11	M(A)

J. Hay & Sons, Ltd.

Alfred Everard	1957	1,543	241	38	10	M(A)
The Duchess	1963	461	170	28	9	M(A)

EVERETT SHIPPING CO. LTD.
Hartlepools

FUNNEL: *Black with yellow letter 'E'.* HULL: *Grey with red boot-topping.*

Irish Trader	1949	365	146	24	9	M(A)
ex Admiral Nelson–70, Admiral Nelson–69						

FAREHAM BALLAST CO. LTD.
Fareham

FUNNEL: *Blue with black top.* HULL: *Grey with black boot-topping.*

Sand Dredgers and Carriers:

Roway	1937	110	90	19	7½	M(A)

FIFE SHIPPING CO. LTD.
London
See D. Cumming & Co. Ltd.

F. T. Everard & Sons Ltd.   M.V. GILLIAN EVERARD

[David W. Jenkins

JAMES FISHER & SONS, LTD.
Barrow

FUNNEL: *Yellow with black top and black letter "F" on broad white band over narrow black band.* HULL: *Black with yellow line and red boot-topping.*

Aberthaw Fisher*	1966	2,355	276	54	11¾	M
Derwent Fisher	1966	1,096	217	34	10½	M(A)
Eden Fisher	1965	1,173	237	35	11	M(A)
Guernsey Fisher †	1971	—	—	—	—	M(A)
Jersey Fisher †	1971	—	—	—	—	M(A)
Kingsnorth Fisher*	1966	2,355	275	54	11¾	M
Orwell Fisher	1968	1,374	296	50	14½	M(A)
Pool Fisher	1959	1,028	218	34	11	M(A)
Solway Fisher	1968	1,374	296	50	14½	M(A)
Seaway Coasters Ltd.						
Brathay Fisher	1971	3,500	—	—	14½	M(A)
Lune Fisher	1962	1,012	218	34	12½	M(A)
International Nuclear Transport Ltd.						
Leven Fisher	1962	1,540	260	39	12½	M(A)
Stream Fisher	1971	—	—	—	14½	M(A)
Anchorage Ferrying Services Ltd.						
Odin	1968	1,844	242	41	9	M(A)

*Heavy Lift Ships on charter to the C.E.G.B.   † Chartered to British Rail

James Fisher & Sons   M.V. KINGSNORTH FISHER   [*John G. Callis*

JOSEPH FISHER & SONS, LTD.
(CAWOOD HOLDINGS LTD.)
Newry

FUNNEL: *Black with red over white over blue band.* HULL: *Black with red boot-topping and dark brown upperworks.*

Olive	...	...	...	...	1963	791	202	33	11	M(A)
Walnut	...	...	...		1955	546	185	28	10	M(A)
	ex Whitehaven–56									

FLEETWOOD SAND & GRAVEL CO. LTD.
Fleetwood

FUNNEL: *Black with yellow over blue over yellow bands.* HULL: *Black with red boot-topping.*

Sand Dredgers and Carriers:									
Bretherdale	...	...	...	1885	435	—	—	—	SR(A)
Pen Itchen**	...	...		1947	399	145	25	8	M(A)

**In Amey Marine colours.

FLEETWOOD TANKERS LTD.
(BOSTON GROUP HOLDINGS LTD.)
Fleetwood

FUNNEL: *Red with black top.* HULL: *Black with red boot-topping.*

Coastal Tankers:									
Onward Enterprise	...	...	1960	334	159	27	10	M(A)	
	ex Dago 2–66, Dago II–66, Mathea–63								
Onward Mariner	...	...	1971	250	131	22	10½	M(A)	
Onward Progress	...	...	1959	345	144	27	9	M(A)	
Onward Voyager	...	...	1971	230	—	—	—	M(A)	

FOLKESTONE SALVAGE CO. LTD.
Folkestone

FUNNEL: *Various.* HULL: *Black.*

Salvage Vessels:									
Kaye Belle	...	...	...	—	178	—	—	9	M(A)
	ex Airmoor–70								
Staley Bridge	...	...		1940	297	138	25	9	M(A)

FOX ELMS, LTD.
Gloucester

FUNNEL: *(None).* HULL: *Black.*

Severn Trader	...	...	...	1932	119	89	19	7½	M(A)

WM. FRANCE, FENWICK & CO. LTD.
London

FUNNEL: *Black with red letters "F F" on broad white band.* HULL: *Black with red boot-topping.*

	Year					
Chelwood	1964	5,440	370	54	13	M(A)
Dalewood	1966	5,390	370	54	13	M(A)
Dartwood	1956	5,720	457	60	12	M(A)
Sherwood	1958	5,279	414	54	12	M(A)
ex Thackeray–68						

G. & H. SHIPPING, LTD.
Kings Lynn

FUNNEL: HULL:

	Year					
Gregham	1950	292	132	23	9	M(A)
ex Reggeborg–70, Skald–54						

J. & A. GARDNER, LTD.
Glasgow

FUNNEL: *Black with white band.* HULL: *Black with white line and green boot-topping, or grey with green or black boot-topping.*

	Year					
Saint Aidan	1962	973	218	34	12	M(A)
Saint Angus	1953	991	224	34	11½	M(A)
ex Milo–69						
Saint Bedan	1972	1,300	—	—	—	M(A)
Saint Colman	1963	975	205	33	12½	M(A)
Saint Fergus	1964	346	143	27	10¼	M(A)
Saint Modan	1960	488	166	27	12	M(A)
Saint Ronan	1966	433	147	28	12	M(A)
Saint William	1967	781	204	32	12	M(A)

GEM LINE, LTD.
(WM. ROBERTSON, SHIPOWNERS, LTD.)
(STEPHENSON CLARKE, LTD.)
Glasgow

FUNNEL: *Black.* HULL: *Black with red boot-topping.*

	Year					
Amber	1956	1,596	268	39	12½	M(A)
Amethyst	1958	1,548	258	40	12	M(A)
Cameo	1952	1,597	275	40	10½	M(A)
ex Gem–60						
Emerald	1952	1,454	241	38	10½	M(A)
Gem	1969	1,599	306	44	12	M(A)
Olivine	1952	1,430	245	38	10¾	M(A)

GEM LINE LTD. *continued*

Pearl	1963	1,093	212	34	10½	M(A)
Sapphire	1966	1,286	228	37	12	M(A)
Topaz	1962	1,597	268	40	13	M(A)
Tourmaline	1962	1,581	268	40	13	M(A)
Scotspark Shipping Co.						
Brilliant	1958	1,143	224	34	11	M(A)

GENERAL STEAM NAVIGATION CO. LTD.
(P. & O. GROUP)
London

FUNNEL: *Black with houseflag (White with red globe surmounting date "1824" in centre and with red letters "G S N C" in each corner.*

HULL: *Black with white line and red boot-topping.*

Albatross	1965	654	214	36	13	M(A)
Avocet	1965	654	214	36	13	M(A)
Petrel	1965	496	160	29	12	M(A)
Normandy Ferries Ltd. (Southern Ferries Ltd., S.A.G.A., and Irish Shipping Ltd.)						
Car and Vehicle Ferries:						
Dragon	1967	5,720	440	72	19	M(2)
Leopard**	1968	5,719	442	72	19	M(2)
Southern Ferries Ltd. (Car and Vehicle Ferries):						
Eagle	1971	11,609	465	72	23	M(2)
Falcon*	1971	1,599	—	—	—	M
Charter Shipping Ltd.						
Tanmarack	1967	1,598	280	42	13	M(A)

*German flag, chartered from J. A. Reinecke, Lubeck. **French flag, owned by S.A.G.A.

ORIOLE .

GEORGE GIBSON & CO. LTD.
Leith

FUNNEL: *Black (with or without the crossed houseflags of the Gibson and Rankin companies).* HULL: *Black with red boot-topping. or red*

Liquefied Gas/Chemical Tankers:						
Dryburgh	1952	1,593	261	38	11¾	M(A)
Ettrick	1957	2,149	297	38	11¾	M(A)
Lanrick	1957	570	244	36	12½	M(A)
Quentin	1940	574	174	28	10½	M(A)
Yarrow	1958	2,148	297	38	11¾	M(A)
Nile Steamship Co. Ltd.						
Teviot	1966	694	186	33	11½	M(A)
Ship Mortgage & Finance Co. Ltd.						
Traquair	1966	699	186	33	11¾	M(A)
Gibson Gas Tankers Ltd.						
Melrose	1971	1,599	261	38	12	M(A)
Deutsche Geo. Gibson & Co. Gastanker GmbH. (German flag):						
Bucklaw	1971	499	—	—	—	M(A)
Durward	1971	499	—	—	12	M(A)

The company also operates chartered Dutch tonnage.

GILLIE & BLAIR, LTD.
Newcastle

FUNNEL: *Black with broad blue band between two narrow white bands.* HULL: *Black with red boot-topping separated by narrow white line.*

Moray Firth IV	1960	613	182	29	10½	M(A)

GLEN & CO. LTD.
Glasgow
See F. T. Everard & Sons Ltd.

Greater London Council   M.V. BEXLEY   *John G. Callis*

GLENLIGHT SHIPPING, LTD.
Glasgow
FUNNEL: *Dark red with black top.*   HULL: *Black with red boot-topping.*

Stormlight	...	...	...	1957	166	—	—	—
Hay Hamilton Ltd.								
Glen Shiel...	...	...	...	1959	195	109	24	9	M(A)
Glenshira	...	...	...	1953	153	86	20	8	M(A)
G. & G. Hamilton Ltd.								
Glencloy	...	...	...	1966	200	109	24	9	M(A)
Glenfyne	...	...	...	1965	200	109	24	9	M(A)
Ross & Marshall Ltd.								
Dawnlight I	...	...	...	1965	199	107	22	9½	M(A)
Fairlight	...	...	...	1966	—	—	—	—	M(A)
Raylight	...	...	...	1963	177	97	21	9	M(A)
Warlight	...	...	...	1932	199	96	23	8½	M(A)

ex Leaspray–66, Goldeve

G. E. GRAY & SONS (SHIPPING) LTD.
(THOS. WATSON (SHPG.) LTD.)
Chatham
FUNNEL: HULL: *Grey with black boot-topping.*

Graybank ...	...	...	1957	382	156	26	10	M(A)
ex Hillswick–68, Greta–64								
Susan	...	...	1957	484	171	28	9	M(A)
ex Jan Brons–65								

GREATER LONDON COUNCIL
London
FUNNEL: *Pale yellow with black top and Council's armorial shield in full colour.*
HULL: *Black with white line and red boot-topping.*

Sludge Carriers:						
Bexley	...	...	...	1966	2,175	295	50	12	M(2A)
Edward Cruse	...	...	1954	1,818	274	44	11	SR(2A)
Hounslow	...	...	1968	2,132	295	50	12	M(2A)
Newham ...			1968	2,175	295	50	12	M(2A)

GREENHITHE LIGHTERAGE CO. LTD.
Greenhithe
FUNNEL: *Yellow.*   HULL: *Green with white line and red boot-topping.*

Ferrocrete	...	...	1927	158	104	21	7	M(A)

GULF SHIPPING LINES, LTD.
London

FUNNEL: HULL:

Gulf Bandar	1962	496	246	35	13	M(A)
ex Baltic–71, Ursula C–66						
Gulf Barat	1952	425	181	28	9½	M(A)
ex Eversand–71, Alice–61						
Gulf Planet	1955	680	199	24	12	M(A)
ex Saint Blane–71						

J. H. K. GRIFFEN
Cardiff

FUNNEL: *White with narrow black top.* HULL: *Black.*

Farringay	1944	461	148	28	8	M(A)
ex Empire Farringay–46 ...						

HADLEY SHIPPING CO. LTD.
London

FUNNEL: *Yellow with black top and black letters "HSC" in white diamond.*
HULL: *Black with red boot-topping.*

Calandria	1969	1,477	253	39	11	M(A)
Camarina	1969	1,473	254	39	12½	M(A)
Corato ...	1969	1,450	253	39	11	M(A)

HALL BROS. STEAMSHIP CO. LTD.
Newcastle

FUNNEL: *Red with black top separated by narrow white over grey over narrow white bands and with replica of houseflag on grey band.* HULL: *Grey with green boot-topping.*

Bretwalda	1971	—	—	—	12	M(A)
Cilurnam	1968	1,432	253	39	12¼	M(A)
Embassage	1968	1,432	253	39	12¼	M(A)
White Crest	1971	1,599	—	—	12	M(A)

HALL (MARINE) LTD.
(READYMIX GROUP)
London

FUNNEL: *Orange with black "Readymix" symbol.* HULL: *Black with red boot-topping.*

Sand Dredgers and Carriers:							
H. W. Wilkinson	1963	188	100	22	7½	M(A)
Harry Ford	1958	132	90	21	6½	M(A)
John Gauntlett	1963	987	100	39	7	M(A)
ex Gritwood–70						
Joseph Hall	1963	187	100	23	7½	M(A)
William Brice	1958	132	90	21	6½	M(A)

R. D. HARBOTTLE & CO. (MERCANTILE) LTD.
London

FUNNEL: *Red with black top separated by white band with "HARDY" in white on black panel superimposed on two red bordered white diamonds.* HULL: *Green with red boot-topping.*

Hardy Merchant	1964	481	165	28	10	M(A)

JOHN HARKER, LTD.
Knottingley

FUNNEL: *Black with red letter "H" in red ring on white panel.* HULL: *Black or black with red boot-topping.*

Bristol Channel, Humber, Mersey and Tyne Coastal Tankers:									
Borrowdale H.	1971	350	—	—	—	M(A)
Deepdale H.	1965	385	153	28	10	M(A)
ex Riverbeacon–67						
Dovedale H.	1962	306	157	22	10	M(A)
ex Riverbridge–67						
Glaisdale H.	1961	303	140	22	9	M(A)
Greendale H.	1962	309	141	22	9	M(A)
Grovedale H.	1966	365	165	22	10	M(A)
Keeldale H.	1962	265	140	22	10	M(A)
Kerrydale H.	1961	255	140	22	10	M(A)
Kingsdale H.	1958	276	140	22	10	M(A)
Kirkdale H.	1957	276	140	22	10	M(A)
Peakdale H.	1968	491	164	22	9	M(A)
Southdale H.	1957	276	140	22	10	M(A)
Teesdale H.	1951	298	152	22	9	M(A)
Tynedale H.	1952	298	152	22	9	M(A)
Weasdale H.	1960	270	135	21	9	M(A)
Wheeldale H.	1953	273	141	22	8	M(A)
Winsdale H.	1962	270	140	22	10	M(A)

Many smaller tank barges on various inland and estuarial waters.

John Harker Ltd. M.V. SOUTHDALE H.

[*P. L. White*]

HARRISONS (CLYDE) LTD.
Glasgow

FUNNEL: *Red with black top.* HULL: *Black with red boot-topping.*

Virgilia	1970	1,437	254	29	12¼	M(A)
Voreda	1969	1,437	254	29	12	M(A)

Both vessels are managed by Chr. Salvesen Ltd.   See also Western Ferries Ltd.

HAY HAMILTON LTD. Glasgow
See Glenlight Shipping Ltd.

HAY & CO. (LERWICK) LTD.
Lerwick

FUNNEL: *Yellow with blue letter "H" on red over white over red bands.*
HULL: *Grey with black boot-topping.*

Shetland Trader	1957	499	178	29	10	M(A)
ex Henriette B.–64						

J. HAY & SONS, LTD. Glasgow
See F. T. Everard & Sons, Ltd.

JOHN HEAVER, LTD.
Littlehampton

FUNNEL: *Grey with narrow black top and blue letters "J H" on broad yellow band.*
HULL: *Grey with black boot-topping.*

Sand Dredgers and Carriers:						
Chichester City	1971	991	196	39	10	M(A)

A. F. HENRY & MACGREGOR, LTD.
Leith

FUNNEL: *Black with two white bands.* HULL: *Black with red boot-topping.*

Cantick Head	1958	1,591	269	40	12	M(A)
Kinnaird Head	1963	1,985	290	42	12½	M(A)
Rattray Head *ANGMERING (GP 2)*	1965	1,600	247	43	10½	M(A)

See also Chr. Salvesen, Ltd.

P. M. HERBERT
(HERB SHIP LTD.)
Bude

FUNNEL: *Yellow with red letter "H".* HULL: *Grey with black boot-topping, or black*

Name				Year					
Arlingham	...	...	...	1934	268	122	22	9	M(A)
	ex Isle of Harris—65, Zeearend—58, Tromp—56, Atlantis—56, Frejo—51, Mr Ham Smeenge—46								
Despatch	...	...	...	1931	199	115	21	7	M(A)
	ex Atlas—37								
Field	...	...	...	1949	133	81	20	8	M(2A)

G. HEYN & SONS, LTD. (HEAD LINE)
Belfast

FUNNEL: *Black with red hand device on blue bordered white shield.* HULL: *Black with red boot-topping.*

Name				Year					
Fair Head	...	...	...	1957	1,948	305	42	12½	M

HINDLEA SHIPPING CO. LTD.
Cardiff

FUNNEL: *Yellow with red letters "HL" on red bordered yellow diamond interrupting red bands.* HULL: *Grey with red boot-topping.*

Name				Year					
Marshlea	...	...	...	1957	495	184	31	11	M(A)

M. F. HORLOCK & CO. LTD.
Mistley

FUNNEL: *(None).* HULL: *Black.*

Name				Year					
Resourceful	...	...	...	1930	100	91	19	7	(M)Aux
Sand Dredgers and Carriers: (M. F. Horlock Dredging Co. Ltd.)									
Adieu	...	...	...	1929	109	93	19	6½	M(Aux)
Reminder	...	...	...	1929	103	93	19	6½	M(Aux)
Spithead	...	...	...	1915	162	111	21	7	M(A)
	ex Admiralty X-Lighter								

HOVERINGHAM GRAVELS LTD.
London

FUNNEL: *Orange-brown with black mastodon device.* HULL: *Black.*

Name				Year					
Sand Dredgers and Carriers:									
Hoveringham I	...	...	...	1966	897	204	36	10	M(A)
Hoveringham III	...	...	...	1954	471	160	31	10	M(A)
	ex Gaist—67								
Hoveringham IV	...	...	...	1969	980	208	60	10	M(A)

HOVERINGHAM GRAVELS LTD. *continued*

Hoveringham V	...	...	1969	879	208	59	11	M(A)
Hoveringham VI	...	...	1972	1,550	—	—	—	M(A)

Hoveringham Dredging Ltd:						
Needwood	1967	1,555	278	46	10	M(A)

HUDSON STEAMSHIP CO. LTD.
London

FUNNEL: *Dark blue with white letter "H" on broad red band.*   HULL: *Black with red boot-topping.*

Hudson River	1949	3,128	337	45	10	SR(A)

J. Hudson Fuel & Shipping Co. Ltd.						
Hudson Light	1965	5,628	370	54	12	M(A)
Hudson Stream*	1971	750	238	43	12½	M(A)

*Effluent Carrier.

HULL GATES SHIPPING CO. LTD.
(BOSTON GROUP HOLDINGS LTD.)
Hull

FUNNEL: *Yellow with narrow black top and houseflag (Red bordered white pennant with red letters "H G".*   HULL: *Blue-grey with green boot-topping, or black with white line and red boot-topping.*

Foxtongate	1963	718	197	30	10	M(A)
Heathergate	1957	597	180	29	9½	M(A)
Irishgate	1965	800	201	32	12	M(A)
Kingsgate	1949	545	182	27	9½	M(A)
Northgate	1964	499	165	29	10	M(A)
Parksgate	1971	798	—	—	—	M(A)
Royalgate	1953	546	189	28	10	M(A)

Coastal Tankers:						
Hullgate	1971	1,594	292	42	12	M(A)
Humbergate	1969	1,579	277	43	12	M(A)

IMPERIAL CHEMICAL INDUSTRIES LTD.
London

FUNNEL: *Blue with black top and "ICI" device in white on red disc.* HULL: *Black with red boot-topping.*

Nobel Division:						
Lady McGowan	1952	690	183	30	10½	M(A)
Lady Roslin	1958	708	175	32	10	M(A)

IMPERIAL CHEMICAL INDUSTRIES *continued*

Mond Division:

Comberbach	...	...	...	1948	201	103	22	8	M(A)
Cuddington	...	...	...	1948	201	103	22	8	M(A)
James Jackson Grundy		...	...	1948	201	103	22	8	M(A)
Marbury	...	...	...	1949	231	105	23	8	M(A)
Marston	...	...	...	1949	231	105	23	8	M(A)
Polythene	...	...	...	1949	330	140	25	9	M(A)
Weaverham	...	...	...	1948	201	103	22	8	M(A)
Wincham	...	...	...	1948	201	103	22	8	M(A)

T. G. IRVING LTD.
Sunderland

FUNNEL: *Black with red star on broad silver band.* HULL: *Black with white top line and green boot-topping.*

Ferndene				1949	313	137	24	9	M(A)

ISLAND TRANSPORT CO. LTD.
Cowes, I.O.W.

FUNNEL: *Yellow with black top.* HULL: *Black with red boot-topping.*

Shalfleet	...	...	...	...	1962	103	96	19	9	M(A)

ISLE OF MAN STEAM PACKET CO. LTD.
Douglas, I.O.M.

FUNNEL: *Red with black top and black rings.* HULL: *Black with red boot-topping separated by white line.*

Passenger Vessels:

Ben-my-Chree**		...	...	1966	2,762	344	53	21	ST(2)
King Orry	...	...	...	1946	2,485	345	47	21	ST(2)
Manx Maid**		...	...	1962	2,724	344	53	21	ST(2)
Manxman	...	...	...	1955	2,495	345	50	21	ST(2)
Mona's Isle	...	...	...	1951	2,491	345	47	21	ST(2)
Mona's Queen**		...	...	1972	—	—	—	—	M(2)
Snaefell	...	...	...	1948	2,489	345	47	21	ST(2)
Tynwald	...	...	...	1947	2,487	345	47	21	ST(2)

Cargo Vessels:

Fenella ..VASSO M (CY) 473				1951	1,019	223	37	12	M
Peveril	...	...	...	1964	1,048	220	41	12	M(A)
Ramsey	...	...	...	1965	446	159	29	12	M(A)

**Car and Vehicle Carriers.

ISLE OF SARK SHIPPING CO. LTD.
(SARK SHIPOWNERS LTD.)
Guernsey, C.I.

FUNNEL: HULL:

Ile de Serk	... ...	1941	195	90	21	8½	M(2)
ex Island Commodore–69							
La Dame de Serk	... ...	1953	152	102	23	8½	M(2)
ex Bateau Morgat–69, Morgat–64							

ISLE OF SCILLY STEAMSHIP CO. LTD.
Penzance

FUNNEL: *Yellow.* HULL: *White with red boot-topping.*

Scillonian ...	... ...	1956	921	210	33	15½	M(2)

JEPPESON—HEATON LTD.
London

FUNNEL: *White with black top and "JH" monogram in black and green.* HULL: *White with green boot-topping.*

Con-Zelo ...	... ...	1957	399	165	26	10	M(A)

JOHN KELLY, LTD.
Belfast

FUNNEL: *Black with red over white over blue bands with a small black letter "K" on the white band.* HULL: *Dark grey with red boot-topping.*

Ballyhill	... ...	1954	986	230	32	10	SR(A)
Ballylesson	... ...	1959	1,280	250	34	11	M(A)
Ballyloran	... ...	1958	1,092	220	34	11	M(A)
Ballymore...	... ...	1950	1,277	244	35	11	M(A)
ex Beeding–70							
Ballyrobert	...	1951	1,473	253	37	10½	M(A)
ex Ardingley–71							
Ballyrory	... ...	1963	1,575	256	39	11½	M(A)
Ballyrush	...	1962	1,575	256	39	11½	M(A)
Ballywalter	... ...	1955	1,637	242	38	10¾	M(A)
ex Steyning–71							

J. Kelly Ltd.   M.V. BALLYHILL   [*David W. Jenkins*

KLONDYKE SHIPPING CO. LTD.
Hull

FUNNEL: *Grey with houseflag* (*Red bordered white swallowtail with black letter* "*K*"). HULL: *Grey or black with red boot-topping.*

Fendyke	...	...	...	1971	890	208	33	12	M(A)
Framptondyke	...	...	...	1964	1,599	281	42	12	M(A)
Kirtondyke	...	...	...	1957	949	215	35	12	M(A)
Somersbydyke	...	...	...	1967	1,599	302	44	11½	M(A)
Westondyke	...	...	...	1971	890	208	33	12	M(A)

J. P. KNIGHT (LONDON) LTD.
London

FUNNEL: *Black with two silver bands and silver letter* "*K*". HULL: *Black.*

Fresh Water Tankers:					
Kingsabbey	1928	351	158	24	7	M(A)
ex Fealtie–66						
Kingsclere	1956	303	139	22	8	M(A)
ex Shell Steelmaker–69						
Kingsthorpe	1956	303	139	22	9	M(A)
ex B.P. Manufacturer–69						

I. P. LANGFORD (SHIPPING) LTD.
Sharpness

FUNNEL: *Red with black top and white letter "L".*   HULL: *Grey with red boot-topping.*

Bristol Channel Tanker:									
Kyles	...	...	...	...	1872*	121	82	18	7	M(A)

*Re-built 1945.

R. LAPTHORN & CO. LTD.
Rochester

FUNNEL: *Red with black band with yellow star superimposed.*   HULL: *Black with grey topsides.*

Hoocrest	...	...	...	...	1955	490	169	27	10	M(A)
ex Ida D.–70										
Hooness	...	...	...	...	1965	196	110	22	8	M(A)
Hootact	...	...	...	...	1950	274	134	23	8½	M(A)
ex Contact–70, Gesina–52										

W. N. LINDSAY (SHIPOWNERS) LTD.
Leith

FUNNEL: *Red with black top separated by blue band.*   HULL: *Black with red boot-topping.*

Rosewell	...	...	...	...	1950	499	163	27	9	M(A)
ex Hotwells–70										
Roseburn	...	...	...	...	1947	604	197	28	9½	M(A)
ex Thorium–64 *STAVROS EMMANUEL (NA)*										

LINK LINES LTD.
Liverpool

FUNNEL: *Black with green edged red chevron.*   HULL: *Black with red boot-topping.*

This company employs tonnage from other Coast Lines Group companies usually carrying Link Lines funnel colours.

LONDON & ROCHESTER TRADING CO. LTD.

Rochester

FUNNEL: *Black with white crescent on broad red band between two narrow white bands.* HULL: *Red brown with white or blue topline and red boot-topping.*

Action	1956	177	95	22	6½	M(A)
Ambience	1969	380	146	26	9	M(A)
Andescol	1961	191	100	22	8	M(A)
Bastion	1958	172	96	22	7	M(A)
Bencol	1964	204	105	23	9	M(A)
Blatence	1969	380	146	26	9	M(A)
Cadence	1969	380	146	26	9	M(A)
Caption	1963	189	105	24	8¼	M(A)
Cecil Gilders	1957	137	91	21	8	M(A)
Crescence	1965	999	221	35	12	M(A)
Dangeld*	1969	694	247	41	13½	M(A)
Dietion	1963	189	105	24	8¼	M(A)
Dominence	1970	425	159	29	10	M(A)
Elation	1963	212	99	22	9	M(A)
Eloquence	1969	380	146	26	9	M(A)
Eminence	1969	999	220	39	10½	M(A)
Faience	1969	424	157	29	10	M(A)
Function	1963	212	100	22	9	M(A)
Gardience	1969	424	157	29	10	M(A)
Gillation	1964	195	102	22	8¼	M(A)
Gold	1951	120	85	20	8	M(A)
Halcience	1970	434	158	29	9	M(A)
Horation	1964	205	106	23	10	M(A)
Ignition	1967	199	105	23	8	M(A)
Josh Francis	1954	137	85	20	6½	M(A)
Jubilation	1967	199	106	23	8½	M(A)
Kiption	1968	196	106	23	8½	M(A)
Libation	1969	198	100	22	8	M(A)
Loach	1968	191	104	22	6¾	M(A)
Lobe	1968	191	104	22	6	M(A)
Locator	1970	194	104	22	6	M(A)
Lodella	1971	200	104	22	6	M(A)
Maguda	1959	170	90	22	8	M(A)
Maloney	1952	124	85	20	7	M(A)
Milligan	1952	124	85	20	7	M(A)
Naughton	1951	120	85	20	6½	M(A)
Niagara	1898	102	86	20	6	M(A)
Nicola Dawn	1955	137	86	21	7	M(A)
Northdown	1924	108	90	21	6	M(A)
Ordinence	1941	325	137	25	9	M(A)
ex Turgail–56, Empire Kyle–46						
Pepita	1955	137	86	21	7½	M(A)
Pertinence	1958	868	206	32	10½	M(A)
Quiescence	1959	868	206	32	10½	M(A)
Resilience†	1969	988	217	37	12¾	M(A)
Resurgence	1958	552	219	33	10½	M(A)
ex Singorita–62, Bermudiana–61, Singorita–58						
Rogul	1965	172	96	22	8	M(A)
Rohoy	1966	172	96	22	8	M(A)
Roina	1966	172	96	22	8	M(A)
Servic	1904	166	90	23	6½	M(A)
Silver	1952	120	85	20	7	M(A)
Spartan	1898	106	85	21	6½	M(A)
Stargate	1926	106	88	21	6	M(A)
ex Wilfred–53						
Thistle	1895	114	86	19	6	M(A)

Also smaller Thames river craft of under 100 g.r.t. †–Starch Carrier. *–White hull.

London & Rochester Trading Co.   M.V. KIPTION

[G. Traill

COMBEN LONGSTAFF & CO. LTD.
London

FUNNEL: *Black with red letters "C L" on white diamond on broad red band.*
HULL: *Black with red boot-topping.*

Caernarvonbrook	1964	1,594	265	39	12	M(A)
Cardiffbrook	—	—	—	—	—	M(A)
Chesterbrook	1964	1,594	265	39	12	M(A)
Clarebrook	1964	1,594	265	39	12	M(A)
Cornishbrook	1961	1,595	260	39	12	M(A)
Dorsetbrook	1957	1,328	235	36	11	M(A)
Warwickbrook	1956	1,036	218	34	11¼	M(A)
Westminsterbrook	1961	1,040	217	34	11	M(A)
Winchesterbrook	1960	1,040	217	34	11¼	M(A)
Worcesterbrook	1958	1,023	218	34	11	M(A)
County Ships Ltd:						
Corkbrook	1964	1,594	265	39	12	M(A)
Somersetbrook	1970	1,596	283	42	12	M(A)
Stirlingbrook	1969	1,596	283	42	12	M(A)
Surreybrook	1970	1,596	283	42	12	M(A)
Sussexbrook	1970	1,596	283	42	12	M(A)

See also the Esk Shipping Co. Ltd.

(1) WESTMINSTERBROOK NOW FAIR JENNIFER (BR)

Comben Longstaff & Co.   M.V. WINCHESTERBROOK   ["*Fotoship*"

M. & G. SHIPPING CO. LTD.
London

FUNNEL: HULL: *Black with red boot-topping.*

Malta Faith	1958	1,334	229	35	11½	M(A)
ex Soutra–69						

MACANDREWS & CO. LTD.
London

FUNNEL: *Yellow.* HULL: *White with green boot-topping.*

Cervantes	1968	1,470	301	44	16½	M(A)
Churruca	1968	1,470	301	44	16½	M(A)
Pacheco	1961	1,242	245	42	16	M(A)
Palacio	1961	1,096	248	42	16	M(A)
Palomares	1963	1,196	245	42	16	M(A)
Sailor Prince	1957	2,055	334	46	14½	M
ex Velarde–69						

DAVID MACBRAYNE, LTD.
(SCOTTISH TRANSPORT GROUP)
Glasgow

FUNNEL: *Red with black top.*   HULL: *Black with red boot-topping and white line.*

Claymore	1955	1,024	192	38	12½	M
Iona	1970	1,150	245	46	16	M(2)
King George V	1926	985	270	32	16	ST(2)
Loch Arkaig	1942	179	113	22	10	M(2)
Loch Carron	1951	683	203	34	11	M(A)
Loch Eynort	1947	117	97	22	8½	M
ex Valonia–62						
Loch Seaforth	1947	1,126	241	36	14	M(2)
ex Empire Maysong–48						
Lochdunvegan	1946	528	190	31	10	M(A)
ex Ornan–50						
Secretary of State for Scotland: Car Ferries:						
Clansman	1964	2,104	235	46	14½	M
Columba	1964	2,104	235	46	14	M
Hebrides	1964	2,104	235	46	14½	M

Under 100 tons: **Lochailort, Lochbuie, Lochnell, Lochshiel and Scalpay.**

P. MacCALLUM & SONS, LTD.
Greenock

FUNNEL: *Red with black top and black rings.*   HULL: *Grey with red boot-topping.*

Ardgarvel	1965	1,121	223	35	11	M(A)
Ardglen	1953	1,044	221	34	10½	M(A)

MALDON SHIPPING CO. LTD.
Maldon

FUNNEL: HULL:

Sand Dredgers and Carriers:							
Bill Brush	1944	192	106	23	7½	M(A)
ex Maureen Brush–69, C.621–61						

CITY OF MANCHESTER (RIVERS DEPT.)
Manchester

FUNNEL: HULL:

Sludge Carrier:						
Mancunian	1946	1,390	263	38	12	M(2A)
Percy Dawson	1968	1,525	258	41	12¾	M(2A)

MANCHE SHIPPING CO. LTD.
Jersey, C.I.

FUNNEL: *Yellow with dark blue band.* HULL: *Grey with black boot-topping.*

Sorel	1958	356	149	24	10	M(A)
ex Lady Sandra–68						

MARDORF PEACH & CO. LTD.
London

FUNNEL: *Yellow "Sunblest" motif on white disc on red funnel with black top separated by white over black bands.* HULL: *Light grey with blue boot-topping.*

Camilla Weston	1966	500	184	29	10½	M(A)
ex Crouch–71						
Catrina Weston	1972	425	—	—	—	M(A)
Gretchen Weston	1966	487	183	29	10½	M(A)
ex Deben–71						
Jana Weston	1972	425	—	—	—	M(A)

MARINE DISPOSALS, LTD.
Lancaster

FUNNEL: *Black with red letters "M D H" on white disc on pale blue band.* HULL: *Black.*

Coastal Tankers:						
Glamardis	1952	262	136	22	8½	M(A)
ex Wandale H.–68						
Marine Fairway	1950	487	—	—	—	M(A)
ex Capcos Lupe–71, Cap Cos–67						
Marine Seaway	1939	369	154	26	8½	M(A)
ex Bridgeman–69, Tripp–50						

MARINEX GRAVELS LTD.
London

FUNNEL: HULL:

Sand Dredgers and Carriers:

Marinex III	1957	554	201	30	10	M(A)
ex Jovista–70, Petro Minor–68, Jovista–66, Thuban–64						
Marinex IV	1970	—	150	—	—	M(A)
Marinex V	1971	2,825	289	53	11½	M(A)

J. MATTHEWS
Liverpool

FUNNEL: *Red with narrow black top and replica of Welsh national flag (Red dragon superimposed on white over green bands).* HULL: *Black with red boot-topping.*

Mertola	1950	497	172	28	9	M(A)
ex Poortvliet–60						

MERRION SHIPPING CO. LTD.
(GILLESPIE & WILLIAMS)
Liverpool

FUNNEL: *Black with broad green band between two narrow white bands with black letters "M S" on yellow disc on green band.* HULL: *Black with red boot-topping, or grey with black boot-topping.*

Isola*	1954	398	162	27	10	M(A)
Olna Firth	1957	591	176	29	10¾	M(A)

*Irish flag

MERSEYSIDE PASSENGER TRANSPORT EXECUTIVE
Liverpool

FUNNEL: *Cream with blue top.* HULL: *Black, red line with red boot-topping.*

Mersey Ferries:

Egremont	1952	566	147	34	12	M(2)
Leasowe	1951	567	147	34	12	M(2)
Mountwood	1960	464	—	—	—	M(2)
Overchurch	1962	468	—	—	—	M(2)
Royal Daffodil	1958	609	159	49	12	M(2)
ex Royal Daffodil II–68						
Royal Iris	1951	1,234	159	48	12	DE(2)
Woodchurch	1960	464	—	—	—	M(2)

METCALF MOTOR COASTERS LTD.
London

FUNNEL: *Green with large white letter "M"*. HULL: *Black or grey with red boot-topping.*

Ann M.	1961	1,203	230	37	11½	M(A)
Christopher M.	1956	1,035	218	34	11	M(A)
David M.	1957	452	166	27	10	M(A)
ex Concorde–70, Rottum–65						
Eileen M.	1966	870	200	35	11½	M(A)
Melissa M.	1956	1,089	230	34	12	M(A)
Michael M.	1955	691	195	31	11	M(A)
Polly M.	1937	380	147	26	8½	M(A)
Thomas M.	1959	398	153	25	10	M(A)
ex Scheldt–70						
Coastal Tankers:						
Frank M.	1965	1,307	232	37	11	M(A)
John M.	1963	1,308	230	37	11	M(A)
Nicholas M.	1966	1,308	232	37	11	M(A)
Wimaisia Shipping Co. Ltd						
Marian M.	1955	694	195	32	11	M(A)
C. Crawley, Ltd. (Water Tanker)						
Aqua	1915	130	105	21	7	M(A)
ex Admiralty X-Lighter						

NELLIE M.

MINISTRY OF DEFENCE
London
(ROYAL MARITIME AUXILIARY SERVICE)

FUNNEL: *Grey with black top.* HULL: *Black.*

Salvage Vessels:						
Barfoot	1942	626	174	32	11½	SR
Barmond	1942	626	174	32	11½	SR
Dispenser	1943	775	179	35	9	SR
Garganey	1966	765	183	37	10	M
Kingarth	1944	775	175	39	9	M
ex Sledway						
Kinloss	1945	775	175	39	9	M
Mandarin	1963	765	183	37	10	M
Succour	1943	775	175	35	9	SR
Sea Salvor	1943	1,212	216	38	12	SR
Uplifter	1943	775	179	35	9	M
Cable Ships:						
Bullfinch	1940	1,524	252	37	12	SR
St Margarets	1943	1,524	252	37	12	SR
Coastal Tanker:						
Eddyfirth (A.261)	1954	2,222	286	44	12	SR(A)
Experimental Vessel:						
Whitehead	—	2,500	329	48	14	M
Stores Carriers:						
Robert Dundas (A.204) ...	1938	1,125	222	35	10½	M(A)
Robert Middleton (A.241) ...	1938	1,087	220	35	10½	M(A)

Metcalf Motor Coasters Ltd.   M.V. FRANK M.   [*David W. Jenkins*

Ministry of Defence (Navy)   M.V. THOMAS GRANT   [*J. Mannering*

(DIRECTOR OF MARINE SERVICES)

FUNNEL: *Yellow with black top with red or blue band between white rings.* HULL: *Black with white topline and red boot-topping.*

Ammunition Carriers:									
Kinterbury	...	...	...	1943	889	200	34	11	SR(A)
Maxim	...	...	...	1944	392	134	25	9	SR(A)
Nordenfelt	...	...	...	1946	392	134	25	9	SR(A)
Throsk	...	...	...	1943	901	200	34	11	SR(A)
Coastal Lubricating Oil Tankers:									
C.632	...	...	...	1948	197	109	22	8	M(A)
C.652	...	...	...	1948	197	109	22	8	M(A)

H. R. MITCHELL & SONS. LTD.
London

FUNNEL: *Yellow with black top.* HULL: *Black or blue with red boot-topping.*

Katherine Mitchell	... ...	1930	177	114	22	8½	M(2A)
May Mitchell	... ...	1950	372	157	23	9½	M(A)
ex Corbiere–71, Lerwick–68, Rema–63							
Patricia Mitchell	... ...	1933	226	128	22	11	M(A)
ex Patricia–68, Britannia–56, Polonia–52, Kragnaes–48, Cranz–47							
Redoubtable	... ...	1915	125	93	23	7	M(Aux)

X JOHN MITCHELL

J. R. L. MOORE
London

FUNNEL: *As Shell-Mex & B.P. Ltd. (On charter).* HULL: *Black.*

Coastal Tanker:							
St. Leonards	... ...	1964	215	117	27	9½	M(A)

W. G. MORAY & CO. LTD.
Garston

FUNNEL: *Yellow with black monogram.* HULL: *Black with green boot-topping.*

Manta	...	...	...	...	1951	366	149	24	10	M(A)

NATIONAL TRUST LTD.
London

FUNNEL: HULL:

Polar Bear	...	...	...	1960	180	113	22	9	M(A)
ex Agdleq–71							

Lundy Island service.

NORTH OF SCOTLAND AND ORKNEYS AND SHETLANDS SHIPPING CO. LTD.
(COAST LINES GROUP)
Aberdeen

FUNNEL: *Yellow.* HULL: *Black with white line and red boot-topping.*

Earl of Zetland	...	...	...	1939	548	166	29	12	M
St. Clair	...	...	...	1960	3,303	296	50	14	M
St. Clement	...	...	...	1946	815	188	31	11½	M(A)
St. Magnus	...	...	...	1955	871	242	36	12½	M(A)
ex City of Dublin–66									
St. Ola	...	...	...	1951	750	178	33	11	M
St. Rognvald	...	...	...	1955	1,024	244	39	13	M(2)

NORTH SEA FERRIES LTD.
(P. & O. GROUP)
Hull

FUNNEL: *Orange.* HULL: *Black with orange line and red boot-topping.*

Norbank*		1962	2,144	258	42	14	M(A)
ex Bison–71							
Norbrae*		1962	2,163	258	43	14	M(A)
ex Buffalo–71							
Car and Vehicle Ferries:							
Norwave	...	...	1965	4,038	357	62	15	M(2)
Norwind†	...	...	1966	4,028	357	62	15	M(2)

*Owned by Coast Lines Ltd. †Owned by Nordzee Veeridensten N.V. Rotterdam (Netherlands flag).

NORTHERN SHIPPING & TRADING CO. (HELMSDALE) LTD.
Aberdeen

FUNNEL: *Black with silver over red over silver bands.* HULL: *Black with red boot-topping.*

Helmsdale	...	...	...	1956	402	153	26	10	M(A)

NORWEST SAND & GRAVEL CO. LTD.
Liverpool

FUNNEL: *Black with red band between two narrow white bands.* HULL: *Black with green boot-topping.*

Sand Dredgers and Carriers:							
Norstar	...	...	...	1961	614	156	36	9	M(A)
Norwest	...	...	...	1955	596	152	35	9½	M(A)

North Sea Ferries Ltd.   M.V. NORWAVE   [*R. J. Weeks*

Orkney Island Shipping Co.   ORCADIA   [*P. Clegg*

OCEAN GAS TRANSPORT LTD.
London

FUNNEL: *Red with black top with white Maltese cross and blue fish device.*   HULL: *Black with red boot-topping.*

Liquefied Gas Tanker:						
Humboldt	1968	5,100	384	54	15	M(A)

FRED OLSEN LINES, LTD.
London

FUNNEL: *Yellow with replica of houseflag (White swallowtail with diagonal blue stripe from top of hoist and blue disc in top of fly).* HULL: *Grey with green boot-topping.*

Blenheim	1970	9,200	490	66	22½	M(A)

British-flag subsidiary company of Fred Olsen, Norway.

ONABI SHIPPING CO.
Hamilton, Bermuda

FUNNEL: *Pale yellow with white letter "T" in white circle on dark blue disc.* HULL: *Black with red boot-topping (Chartered to A/S Terkol, Aarhus, Norway).*

Oil/Chemical Tankers:						
Odabo	1972	499	—	—	—	M(A)
Onabi	1968	565	210	32	11½	M(A)
Bobodi Shipping Ltd:						
Bobodi	1968	699	228	39	12	M(A)

ORKNEY ISLANDS SHIPPING CO. LTD.
Kirkwall

FUNNEL: *Red with white "OI" monogram between two narrow white bands.* HULL: *Black with red boot-topping.*

Islander	1969	250	132	32	11	M(2A)
Orcadia*	1963	896	164	37	12	M(A)

*Owned by Secretary of State for Scotland.

T. J. PALMER & SONS
Gravesend

FUNNEL: *Blue with narrow black top and white letter "P".* HULL: *Dark green with red boot-topping.*

Glas Island	1935	211	104	24	7	M(2A)
ex Lady Stella–55						
Lafford	1958	138	90	21	8	M(A)
Thuroklint	1962	299	—	—	—	M(A)

R. & W. PAUL (MALTSTERS) LTD.
Ipswich

FUNNEL: *None.* HULL: *Black.*

Jock	1908	106	90	21	8	M(Aux)
Lady Daphne	1923	117	90	21	8	M(Aux)
Lady Jean	1926	118	90	22	8	M(Aux)

Also smaller auxiliary-powered barges.

PEACOCK SHIPPING LTD.
Guernsey

FUNNEL: *Red with black top and houseflag.* HULL: *Peacock blue with gold line and red boot-topping.*

Kilbride	1942	321	137	28	9	M(A)
ex Chassiron–51, Orsoto–49, Westerhaven–46, Empire Reynard–44						

PRINCE LINE LTD.
(FURNESS WITHY GROUP)
London

FUNNEL: *Black with narrow red band over broad red band with white Prince of Wales feathers.* HULL: *Black with red boot-topping.*

Chiltern Prince	1970	1,499	285	47	13½	M(A)
Cotswold Prince...	1970	1,460	285	47	13½	M(A)
Malvern Prince	1970	1,459	285	47	13½	M(A)
Mendip Prince	1970	1,459	285	47	13½	M(A)
Pennine Prince	1971	—	—	—	—	M(A)

J. J. PRIOR (TRANSPORT) LTD.
London

FUNNEL: *Red with black top.* HULL: *Black.*

Sand Carriers:						
A.H.P.	1917	175	—	—	7	M(A)
ex Admiralty X-Lighter						
Bert Prior...	1965	175	—	—	9½	M(A)
Colne Trader	1941	329	136	25	9	M(A)
ex Walcrag–62, Springcrag–54, Empire Crag–46						
James P.	1963	191	—	—	8	M(A)
Leah P.	1915	172	—	—	7	M(A)
ex Betty Hudson–64						
Leonard P.	1915	174	—	—	7	M(A)
ex James M.–64 (Admiralty X-Lighter)						
Peter P.	1915	186	—	—	6½	M(A)
Sidney P.	1916	162	—	—	7	M(A)
ex Sway–64 (Admiralty X-Lighter)						

RAMSEY SHIPPING CO. LTD.
Ramsey, I.O.M.

FUNNEL: *Black with white Maltese cross on red band.* HULL: *Grey with red boot-topping.*

Ben Rein	1947	407	149	26	10	M(A)
ex Tamara–56, Lita–54						
Ben Varrey	1963	451	170	28	10¾	M(A)
Ben Veen	1965	485	161	29	12	M(A)
ex Plover–71						
Ben Veg	1965	346	144	26	8½	M(A)
Ben Vooar	1950	427	160	27	8½	M(A)
ex Mudo–59						

RISDON BEAZLEY, ULRICH HARMS, LTD.
Southampton

FUNNEL: *Yellow with black grapnel, with or without black top.* HULL: *Black with red boot-topping.*

Salvage Craft, etc.:						
Droxford	1958	1,302	226	37	11½	SR(A)
Queen Mother	1944	184	102	23	9	M(A)
Topmast 18	1942	497	195	31	7½	M(2A)
ex Rampino–64						
Topmast 20	1942	485	204	31	7½	M(2A)
Twyford	1952	1,104	221	36	12	SR(A)
Risdon A. Beazley:						
Topmast 16	1943	434	192	30	5	M(2A)
ex Segundo–64						
Lifeline	1944	783	179	36	9¾	M

J. R. RIX & SONS, LTD.
Hull

FUNNEL: *Red with black top separated by blue band with white "J R" monogram on red diamond. (Whitehaven Shpg. Co. vessels have blue bordered red diamond).* HULL: *Green with white topline and red boot-topping.*

Fylrix	1962	637	189	28	10½	M(A)
Rix Shipping Co. Ltd.						
Jonrix	1957	647	202	29	10½	M(A)
Whitehaven Shipping Co. Ltd.						
Kenrix	1960	635	204	28	10½	M(A)
Lesrix	1957	676	185	33	10½	M(A)
ex Whitehaven–63						
Highseas Ltd :						
Bobrix	1957	584	180	29	10	M(A)

ROSS & MARSHALL, LTD.
Glasgow
· See Glenlight Shipping Ltd.

C. ROWBOTHAM SONS (MANAGEMENT) LTD.
London

FUNNEL: *Yellow with narrow black top and red letter "R".* HULL: *Black with red boot-topping.*

Coastal Tankers:

Anchorman	...	...	...	1962	795	203	31	$10\frac{3}{4}$	M(A)
Chartsman	...	...	...	1967	787	203	31	10	M(A)
Guidesman	...	...	...	1964	799	203	31	$10\frac{1}{2}$	M(A)
Helmsman	...	...	...	1971	3,800	—	—	—	M(A)
Leadsman	...	...	...	1968	843	205	33	11	M(A)
Oarsman	...		...	1959	778	204	31	10	M(A)
Pointsman	...	...	...	1970	2,886	325	47	12	M(A)
Rudderman	...	...	...	1968	1,592	274	41	12	M(A)
Steersman	...	...	...	1971	1,567	274	41	12	M(A)
Tillerman	...	...	...	1963	807	203	31	10	M(A)
Wheelsman	...	...	...	1967	2,897	322	47	$12\frac{3}{4}$	M(A)

RYE SHIPPING LTD.
Rye

FUNNEL: HULL:

Maralie ... ... ex Hollandia–71, Holland–62	1951	327	143	24	$8\frac{1}{2}$	M(A)
Reedwarbler ... ... ex Ancora–60, Fiat–55	1951	375	148	25	10	M(A)
Rye Trader ... ... ex Polarlight–69, Queensgate–65	1959	200	118	25	$9\frac{1}{2}$	M(A)

SAND SUPPLIES (WESTERN) LTD.
Bristol

FUNNEL: *Black with black letters "SS" superimposed on red bordered white letter "W".* HULL: *Black with red boot-topping.*

Sand Dredgers and Carriers:

Sand Gem ... ... ex Jersey Castle–70, Wimborne–68	1949	313	147	25	$9\frac{1}{2}$	M(A)
Sand Jade ... ... ex Auriga G.–71, Auriga–54	1954	398	160	27	$9\frac{1}{2}$	M(A)
Sand Pearl ... ... ex Wycliff–70	1949	113	100	18	8	M(A)
Sand Topaz ... ... ex Denby–70	1938	108	99	18	8	M(A)

CHRISTIAN SALVESEN, LTD.
Leith

FUNNEL: *Red with blue top separated by broad white band.* HULL: *Black with red boot-topping.*

Duncansby Head*	...	...	1969	4,440	369	52	12¾	M(A)
Dunvegan Head*	...	...	1960	4,300	362	52	12½	M(A)
Tod Head*	...	...	1971	1,599	—	—	—	M(A)
Troop Head	...	...	1971	1,599	—	—	—	M(A)

*In A. F. Henry & Macgregor colours.

SCOTTISH MALT DISTILLERS LTD.
Edinburgh

FUNNEL: *Yellow.* HULL: *Black with red boot-topping.*

Pibroch	...	...	...	...	1957	157	87	20	9½	M(A)

SEA & CONTINENTAL WATERWAYS
TRANSPORT CO. LTD.
London

FUNNEL: HULL:

Sea Rhine	...	...	1970	198	147	24	10	M(A)
Sea Trent	...	...	...	1971	200	146	24	10	M(A)

ex Seacon–71

SEA CONTAINERS LTD.
Liverpool

FUNNEL and HULL: *Usually those of the chartering company.*

Atlantic Bermudian	...	...	1971	1,590	280	45	16	M(A)
Atlantic Jamaican	...	...	1971	1,590	280	45	16	M(A)
England	...	...	1970	930	280	45	16	M(A)
Minho	...	...	1969	930	280	45	16	M(A)
Tagus	...	...	...	1970	930	280	45	16	M(A)
Tamega	...	...	1971	1,598	280	45	16	M(A)
Tiber	...	...	...	1970	1,590	280	45	16	M(A)
Tormes	...	...	...	1970	930	280	45	16	M(A)
Tronto	...	...	...	1971	1,578	279	45	16	M(A)
Tua	...	...	...	1970	930	280	45	16	M(A)
Vento di Maestrale	...	...	1971	1,600	284	45	16	M(A)
Vento di Scirocco	...	...	1971	1,600	284	45	16	M(A)
Voorloper	...	...	1971	1,600	284	45	16	M(A)

SHAMROCK SHIPPING CO. LTD.
Larne

FUNNEL: *Red with black top separated by blue band bearing white letter "S", but usually those of the chartering company.* HULL: *Black with red boot-topping.*

Clonlee*	1959	643	183	32	10½	M(A)
ex Calcium–65						
Curran	1967	1,325	229	36	12	M(A)
Moyle	1967	1,325	229	36	12	M(A)

*Irish flag.

SHAW SAVILL & ALBION CO. LTD.
(FURNESS WITHY GROUP)
London

FUNNEL: *Generally that of operating company which may or may not be the above.* HULL: *Black with white line and red boot-topping.*

Cairnventure	1969	1,430	253	39	12	M(A)
Saxon Prince	1971	1,599	262	39	12	M(A)
Launched as *Cairntrader*.						

H. K. SHAW
Gloucester

FUNNEL: *Blue.* HULL: *Grey with black boot-topping.*

Fretherne	1950	351	147	23	8½	M(A)
ex Eagle–2 71, Merwestad–69, Favoriet–55, Campen–54						

A. H. SHEAF & CO. LTD.
Newport, I.O.W.

FUNNEL: HULL:

Ash Lake	1939	201	124	22	9	(M(A))
ex Dina–69, Mitropa–40						

SHELL-MEX & B.P. LTD.
London

FUNNEL: *Black with yellow band between two white bands.* HULL: *Black, or black with red boot-topping.*

Coastal Tankers:						
Ardrossan	1968	1,529	249	41	11	M(A)
B. P. Haulier	1955	315	148	29	7½	M(A)
Ben Bates	1956	565	181	28	10½	M(A)
Ben Harold Smith	1952	325	136	26	8½	M(A)
Ben Hittinger	1951	522	181	28	9½	M(A)

SHELL-MEX & B.P. LTD. *continued*

British Toiler				1925	131	109	23	7½	M(A)
Caernarvon	...	...	...	1971	—	—	—	—	M(A)
Dingle Bank				1966	1,176	216	37	10½	M(A)
Dublin				1963	1,077	215	37	11	M(A)
Dundee	...	...	...	1971	—	—	—	—	M(A)
Falmouth				1965	982	202	34	10½	M(A)
Grangemouth	...	...	...	1968	1,529	249	41	11	M(A)
Hamble	...		...	1964	1,182	215	37	10½	M(A)
Inverness	...			1968	1,529	249	41	11½	M(A)
Killingholme	...	...	...	1964	1,182	215	37	10½	M(A)
Pando	...	...	...	1967	587	171	35	9½	M(A)
Partington	...	...	...	1965	982	202	34	10½	M(A)
Perfecto	...	...	...	1967	588	172	35	9½	M(A)
Perso	...	...	...	1967	620	171	35	9½	M(A)
Plymouth	...	...	...	1971	—	—	—	—	M(A)
Poilo	...	...	...	1967	620	171	35	9½	M(A)
Point Law				1967	1,529	249	41	11	M(A)
Pronto	...	...	...	1967	588	172	35	9½	M(A)
Shell Dispenser	...	...		1963	239	133	27	9½	M(A)
Shell Farmer	...	...		1955	313	145	30	8	M(A)
Shell Welder	...	...	...	1956	569	171	30	8½	M(A)
Swansea	...	...	...	1971	—	—	—	—	M(A)
Teesport	...	...	...	1966	1,175	215	37	10½	M(A)
Torksey	...	...	...	1964	215	117	27	9½	M(A)

Coastal tankers in Shell colours are operated by a number of other companies on charter.

Shell-Mex & B.P. Ltd.   M.V. DINGLE BANK   [*R. J. Weeks*

SHIPPING & COAL CO. LTD.
London

FUNNEL: *Black with blue diamond on broad white band between two narrow red bands.* HULL: *Black with red boot-topping.*

Greenland...	1962	2,200	285	43	14½	M(A)
Queensland	1958	2,750	336	45	12	M(A)
ex Greathope–64						

SILVER CHEMICAL TANKERS, LTD.
London

FUNNEL: *Black with houseflag (White with blue panel containing two white diagonal stripes between narrow white bars) on white panel.* HULL: *Dark blue with red boot-topping.*

Chemical Tankers:

Silvereid*	1969	1,596	300	40	13	M(A)
Silvereagle	1971	4,039	346	54	13¾	M(A)
Silverfalcon	1966	1,301	254	41	12	M(A)
Silverharrier**	1971	4,622	351	55	13¾	M(A)
Silverkestrel	1965	456	186	31	12	M(A)
Silvermerlin†	1968	1,259	254	41	12	M(A)
Silverosprey	1971	4,038	346	54	13¾	M(A)

*Owned by Wm. Brandts (Leasing) Ltd. **Owned by Ship Mortgage Finance Co. Ltd.
†Owned by John I. Jacobs & Co. Ltd.

R. P. SLACK
Fareham

FUNNEL: *(None).* HULL: *Dark grey with black boot-topping.*

Sand Dredgers and Carriers:

Bloors	1945	245	147	22	8	M(A)

SOUTH COAST SHIPPING CO. LTD.
Southampton

FUNNEL: *Black with black diamond on broad white band.* HULL: *Black with red boot-topping.*

Sand Dredgers and Carriers:

Sand Finch	1958	478	165	27	10	M(A)
ex Ron Woolaway–70, Selskar–60						
Sand Grebe	1959	531	174	30	9	M(A)
Sand Gull	1964	534	174	30	9½	M(A)
Sand Lark	1963	540	174	30	9½	M(A)
Sand Martin	1936	633	177	29	9	M(A)
ex Rookwood–51						
Sand Skua	1971	1,180	—	—	9½	M(A)
Sand Snipe	1961	517	174	30	9½	M(A)
Sand Swan	1969	1,162	218	41	9½	M(A)
Sand Swift	1969	1,085	218	41	9½	M(A)
Sand Tern	1964	535	174	30	9	M(A)
Sand Wren	1943	309	141	21	—	M(A)
ex Pen Adur–69, Lerryn, Morton Corbett						

R.M.C. Management Services Ltd.

Sand Wader	1970	3,270	316	56	—	M(2A)

Silver Chemical
Tankers Ltd.
M.V. SILVER-
KESTREL
["Fotoship"]

South Coast
Shipping Co.
M.V. SAND
SNIPE
[John G. Callis]

SOUTHAMPTON, ISLE OF WIGHT & SOUTH OF ENGLAND ROYAL MAIL STEAM PACKET CO. LTD.
Southampton

FUNNEL: *Red with black top.* HULL: *Black with white upperworks and red boot-topping.*

Car and Vehicle Ferries:								
Carisbrooke Castle	...	...	1959	672	191	42	14	M(2)
Cowes Castle	...	...	1965	786	191	42	14	M(2)
Norris Castle	...	...	1968	734	191	42	14	M(2)
Osborne Castle ...	...	...	1962	736	191	42	14	M(2)

SOUTHERN TANKER & BUNKERING CO. LTD.
Southampton

FUNNEL: *Yellow with houseflag (Yellow letters "S T B C" in each corner of blue field with black "&" in white diamond between two black edged white bands.* HULL: *Dark grey with red boot-topping, or black.*

Coastal Tankers:							
Easternstan	1951	234	137	21	8	M(A)
ex Wyesdale H.–70						
Florencestan	1949	582	199	28	8	M(A)
ex Thorwald–68, Vigilanter–55, Noord–55						
Mabelstan	1949	696	195	30	11½	M(A)
ex Jill.–69, Sylvia–64, Margit Reuter–50						
Northernstan	1971	—	—	—	—	M(A)
Southernstan	1956	303	139	22	8	M(A)
ex Shell Roadbuilder–70						
Westernstan	1947	220	135	21	8½	M(A)
ex Westernstan H.–68						

SOUTHWOLD MARINE AGGREGATES LTD.
Wickford

FUNNEL: HULL:

Sand Dredgers and Carriers:						
Calyx	1929	212	109	21	8½	M(A)
ex Alcyon–36, Eems–35						
Careyna	1949	211	105	22	—	M(A)
ex Constellation–68, Comity–64, C.648–58						

SPRINGWELL SHIPPING CO. LTD.
(T. E. KETTLEWELL & SONS)
Hull

FUNNEL: *Red with yellow star superimposed on black band.* HULL: *Black with red boot-topping.*

Hoofinch	1964	332	145	26	9½	M(A)
ex Springfinch–68						

STEPHENSON CLARKE SHIPPING LTD.

London

FUNNEL: *Black with broad silver band.* HULL: *Black with white topline, red boot-topping and brown upperworks.*

Amberley	1953	1,934	262	39	10½	M(A)
Arundel	1956	3,422	344	46	10½	SR(A)
Ashington	1957	3,894	357	50	11	M(A)
ex Tennyson–68						
Beeding	1971	1,600	—	—	—	M(A)
Birling**	1950	1,771	271	40	10	M(A)
ex Thomas Hardie–68						
Brightling	1952	2,002	272	39	10	M(A)
ex Corbrae–71						
Climping	1958	1,877	275	39	11	M(A)
ex Camberwell–69						
Ferring	1969	1,596	285	43	12½	M(A)
Findon	1957	3,432	344	46	10½	M(A)
ex Rondo–61 *INDON (CY) 1973*						
Fletching	1958	1,877	275	39	11	M(A)
ex Ewell–70						
Harting**	1953	1,799	271	40	10	M(A)
ex Thomas Livesey–69						
Jevington	1959	5,330	414	54	12½	M(A)
ex Macaulay–68						
Keynes**	1950	1,771	271	40	11	M(A)
ex Accum–67						
Kylebank	1961	1,143	228	36	11	M(A)
Lancing	1958	1,765	262	38	10½	M(A)
Malling	1969	1,596	285	43	12½	M(A)
Portslade ...	1955	1,797	242	40	11	M(A)
Pulborough ...	1965	4,995	370	53	12½	M(A)
Rogate	1967	4,997	370	53	12½	M(A)
Shoreham	1957	1,834	262	40	12	M(A)
Steyning	1965	1,594	265	39	—	M(A)
ex Glanton–71						
Storrington	1959	3,809	345	49	11	M(A)
Tarring	1958	1,877	275	39	11	M(A)
ex Lambeth–70						
Totland	1952	1,570	241	38	11½	M(A)
Wadhurst	1962	3,914	375	49	12	M(A)
ex Saphir–70						
Wilmington	1969	5,689	410	55	13	M(A)
Worthing	1957	1,873	275	39	11	M(A)
ex Dulwich–70						
Coastal Tankers:						
Fernhurst	1961	1,525	260	40	10½	M(A)
Firle	1958	948	211	35	9	M(A)
Friston	1959	948	211	34	9½	M(A)
Maplehurst	1961	1,331	230	40	10½	M(A)
Midhurst	1960	1,525	260	40	10½	M(A)
Petworth	1958	1,266	234	35	10½	M(A)
Stansted	1957	1,034	223	34	10½	M(A)
Hopper Barges, Sludge Carriers, etc:						
Megstone	1946	988	207	35	8½	SR(A)
ex Cargo Fleet No 3–72						
David Marley	1963	730	182	37	9½	M(A)
Falstone	1934	359	131	27	8½	M(A)
ex Amsterdam VI						
Adderstone	1950	814	185	36	11¾	M(A)
ex Springwood–72						

JOHN STEWART & CO. (SHIPPING) LTD.
Glasgow

FUNNEL: *Black with broad blue band between two narrow white bands.* HULL: *Black with red boot-topping.*

Yewarch	1957	967	214	35	12	M(A)
ex Ninrich Sieghold–60						
Yewforest	1958	1,097	222	35	10½	M(A)
Yewglen	1960	1,323	230	35	12½	M(A)
ex Tolsta–70						
Yewhill	1957	1,089	221	35	10½	M(A)
Yewkyle	1960	1,323	230	35	12½	M(A)
ex Laksa–71						
Yewmount	1955	1,031	221	34	10½	M(A)
Yewtree	1954	1,114	218	35	10	M(A)
ex Irish Fern–64						

SULLY & STREVENS
Sittingbourne

FUNNEL: *None.* HULL: *Black.*

Beatrice Maud	1910	102	88	21	8	M(Aux)
Hydrogen	1906	124	94	22	7	M(Aux)
Peter Robin	1916	156	105	21	7½	M(A)
ex Admiralty X-Lighter						
Phoenician	1922	104	85	21	6	M(A)
Trilby	1896	153	96	23	7¾	M(Aux)
Sully Bros. & T. J. Palmer:						
Subro Venture	1971	196	—	—	9	M(A)

TANKERS, LTD.
Liverpool

FUNNEL: HULL:

Athelsprite	1971	700	196	34	—	M(A)

TAY SAND CO. LTD.
(D. DAVIDSON)
Dundee

FUNNEL: *Black with houseflag (white with two interlocking black diamonds).*
HULL: *Black or grey with red boot-topping.*

Sand Dredgers and Carriers:						
Middlebank	1935	324	136	25	9	M(A)
ex The Marchioness–66, Camroux II–60						
Rayjohn	1931	155	105	22	7	M(A)

TEES MARINE SERVICES, LTD.
Middlesbrough
FUNNEL: *Red.*   HULL: *Black with red boot-topping.*

Teessider III	1948	365	148	25	8½	M(A)
ex Neptunus–71						
Teessider V	—	—	—	—	—	M(A)
ex Stadland–71						

TEXACO OVERSEAS TANKSHIPS LTD.
London
FUNNEL: *Black with "TEXACO" badge on broad green band.*   HULL: *Black with red boot-topping.*

Coastal Tanker:

Texaco Whitegate	1952	2,022	260	45	11	M(A)
ex Caltex Whitegate–66 Caltex Pakenbaru–59						
Texaco Gloucester*	1959	12,834	—	—	—	SR(2A)

*Ocean Tanker employed in coastal trades.

THUN TANKERS, LTD.
Newcastle
FUNNEL: HULL: Grey

Oil/Chemical Tankers:

Thuntank 5	1968	2,901	322	47	12¾	M(A)
Thuntank 6	1969	3,000	322	47	12¾	M(A)

Other numbered 'Thuntank' vessels are Norwegian owned and operate under that country's flag.

TOWER SHIPPING CO. LTD.
London
FUNNEL: *Dark blue with white tower device.*   HULL: *Grey with red boot-topping.*

Tower Conquest	1968	200	137	25	9	M(A)
Tower Duchess	1969	200	137	25	9	M(A)
Tower Marie	1969	199	137	25	9	M(A)
Tower Princess	1969	200	137	25	9	M(A)
Tower Venture	1969	200	137	25	9	M(A)
Tower Helen	1971	425	—	—	—	M(A)

TOWER

TOWNSEND CAR FERRIES LTD.
Dover

FUNNEL: *Red with black top.*   HULL: *Light green with red boot-topping.*

Car and Vehicle Ferries:

Autocarrier*	1948	1,528	288	53	19	M(2)
ex Royal Sovereign–67						
Free Enterprise I	1962	2,607	316	54	18	M(2)
ex Free Enterprise–64						
Free Enterprise II*	1965	4,122	355	60	19	M(2)
Free Enterprise III*	1966	4,657	385	63	20	M(2)
Free Enterprise IV	1969	5,049	385	64	$20\frac{3}{4}$	M(2)
Free Enterprise V	1970	5,044	386	64	$20\frac{3}{4}$	M(2)

Operated by P. & A. Campbell Ltd. (White funnels, black hulls).

Balmoral	1949	688	204	32	$14\frac{1}{2}$	M(2)
St Trillo	1936	314	149	27	13	M(2)
ex St Sirio–45						
Westward Ho	1938	600	200	30	15	M(2)
ex Vecta–66						

*Owned by the Stanhope S.S. Co.

Free Enterprise VI
✗ Free Enterprise VII

Townsend Car Ferries Ltd.   M.V. FREE ENTERPRISE IV   [*J. Mannering*

TRIPORT SHIPPING CO. LTD.
(J. & J. DENHOLM MANAGEMENT LTD.)
London

FUNNEL: *White with black wheel and blue wave device.* HULL: *Blue with red boot-topping.*

Tor Gothia	1971	—	—	—	—	M2(A)
Tor Mercia	1969	1,600	360	64	12	M2(A)
Tor Scandia	1969	1,600	360	64	12	M2(A)

The larger **Tor Anglia and Tor Hollandia** are Swedish owned and operate under that country's flag.

TURNBULL, SCOTT MANAGEMENT LTD.
London

FUNNEL: *Black with white letters "TS" in white-bordered red shield.* HULL: *Black with red boot-topping.*

Turnbull, Scott Shipping Co. Ltd.						
Redgate	1968	1,426	254	39	11¼	M(A)
Saltersgate	1968	1,426	253	39	11¼	M(A)
Trongate	1968	1,432	253	39	11¼	M(A)
ex Holland Park–71						
Waynegate	1971	1,600	278	43	12	M(A)
Park Steamship Ltd. (Funnel: Dark green with white 'PS' monogram).						
Hyde Park	1968	1,426	253	39	11½	M(A)
Tere	1970	1,598	276	39	12¾	M(A)

TYNE-TEES STEAM SHIPPING CO. LTD.
(COAST LINES GROUP)
Newcastle

FUNNEL: *Black with white over red bands.* HULL: *Black with white line.*

Stormont	1954	906	226	36	12	M(A)
ex Fruin–63, Fife Coast–58						
Yorkshire Coast	1959	785	196	33	11	M(A)

UNIVERSAL WELDING & CONSTRUCTION CO. LTD.
London

FUNNEL: HULL:

Tairlaw	1941	187	123	22	9	M(A)
ex Tim–67, Walcheren						

UNILEVER MERSEYSIDE LTD.
Liverpool

FUNNEL: *Red with black top.*   HULL: *Black with red boot-topping.*

Name									
Laundola	...	...	...	...	1947	199	100	23	8	M(A)
Lifebuoy	...	...	...	...	1949	198	101	23	8¼	M(A)
Lobol	...	...	...	...	1941	200	101	23	8¼	M(A)
Lux	...	...	...	...	1950	205	100	23	8½	M(A)
Rinso	...	...	...	...	1947	198	101	23	8¼	M(A)

UNITED BALTIC CORPORATION LTD.
London

FUNNEL: *Pale yellow with narrow black top and houseflag device on black-edged white disc.*   HULL: *Grey with green boot-topping.*

Name				Year					
Baltic Arrow	...	...	...	1956	1,385	291	41	14½	M(2)
Baltic Express	...	...	...	1957	1,836	334	46	15¾	M(2)
Baltic Jet	...	...	...	1959	1,481	299	42	14	M(A)
Baltic Sprite	...	...	...	1960	960	263	41	13	M(A)
Baltic Star	...	...	...	1961	1,571	305	42	14	M(A)
Baltic Sun REEFER CITY (SG)				1962	3,505	390	56	15½	M(2)
Baltic Swift FIJIAN SWIFT (IR)				1957	1,224	291	41	13	M(2A)
Baltic Valiant	...	...	...	1969	2,125	339	52	14	M(A)
Baltic Vanguard	...	...	...	1966	1,903	308	49	15	M(A)
Baltic Venture	...	...	...	1965	1,581	332	46	13½	M(2)
Baltic Viking	...	...	...	1967	698	245	41	14	M(A)
BALTIC ENTERPRISE				1972	4469				M

VECTIS SHIPPING CO. LTD.
Newport, I.O.W.

FUNNEL: *Yellow with red letters "VSC".*   HULL: *Grey with yellow line and black boot-topping.*

Name				Year					
Gazelle	...	...	...	1904	166	90	23	8	M(2A)
ex Goldrune–51, Runic–49									
Murius	...	...	...	1962	125	97	20	8	M(2A)
Newclose	...	...	...	1960	118	98	20	7	M(2A)
Oceanic	...	...	...	1903	158	90	23	7	M(2A)
Riverclose	...	...	...	1957	110	90	20	8	M(2A)
Seaclose	...	...	...	1954	110	90	20	8	M(2A)

VAN BROEK MARINE (SHIPPING) LTD.
London

FUNNEL: HULL: *Grey with black boot-topping.*

Name				Year					
Edna B.	...	...	...	1938	242	127	23	8	M(A)
ex Annie G.–70, Brandaris–54									

THOMAS WATSON (SHIPPING) LTD.
Rochester

FUNNEL: *Yellow with blue band between two red bands.*   HULL: *Blue with red boot-topping.*

Lady Sabina	1952	410	149	24	9	M(A)
ex Glencullen–68, Walcheren–64						
Lady Sandra	1970	199	137	25	9	M(A)
Lady Sarita	1965	200	136	25	9	M(A)
Lady Serena	1964	200	137	25	8¾	M(A)
Lady Sheena	1966	200	136	25	9	M(A)
Lady Sybilla	1952	325	149	24	10	M(A)
Downlands Shipping Inc, (Liberian flag):						
Lady Sophia	1964	596	—	—	—	M(A)
ex Shannon–70						

WESTERN DREDGERS LTD.
Cardiff

FUNNEL: *Yellow with black top.* HULL: *Black.*

Sand Dredgers and Carriers:						
Instow	1964	735	—	—	—	M(A)
Isca	1960	550	—	—	—	M(A)
Moderator	1965	836	—	—	—	M(A)

WESTERN FERRIES LTD.
Glasgow

FUNNEL: *White with red wheel and arrow device on superstructure.* HULL: *Red.*

Car and Vehicle Ferries:						
Sound of Ghia	—	—	—	—	—	M(2A)
Sound of Islay	1968	280	142	31	10¾	M(2)
Sound of Jura	1969	600	162	36	14	M(2)

WESTERN SHIPPING LTD.
Jersey, C.I.

FUNNEL: *Blue with white band and the letters "W S" in blue pm white diamond.* HULL: *Dark blue with red boot-topping.*

Treviscoe	1952	494	172	28	10½	M(A)
ex Lijnbaansgracht–62						

F

WESTMINSTER GRAVELS LTD.
Southampton

FUNNEL: *Black or grey with blue over yellow houseflag.* HULL: *Black or grey with red boot-topping.*

Sand Dredgers and Carriers:

Bankstone...	1949	1,357	235	36	9½	M(A)
ex Hydracrete–63, Poole Island–59						
Norstone	1964	1,599	276	39	12	M(A)
ex Konsul Retzlaff–70						
Rockstone	1907	842	204	32	9	M(A)
ex James No 47–64, P.L.A. Hopper No 8, Thames Conservancy Hopper No 8.						
Seastone	1907	861	204	32	9	M(A)
ex James No 46–61, P.L.A. Hopper No 7, Thames Conservancy Hopper No 7.						
Wightstone	1950	1,313	235	36	9¼	M(A)
ex Brentford–61, Brent Knoll–61						

X DEEPSTONE

WEST WALES STEAMSHIP CO. LTD.
Newport, (Mon.)

FUNNEL: *Red with black top.* HULL: *Grey with black boot-topping.*

Dolphin G.	1958	500	—	—	10	M(A)
ex Martinistad–71						

WHARF HOLDINGS LTD.
London

FUNNEL: *Black.* HULL: *Black.*

Thames Tankers:

Astro	1964	551	176	34	10	M(A)
B.P. Spirit	1939	440	162	32	8½	M(A)
Banco	1967	544	176	34	8½	M(A)
Hero	1957	967	217	32	11	M(A)
ex Adrian M–71						
Petro	1939	444	162	32	8½	M(A)
Shell Spirit 1	1938	440	162	32	8½	M(A)
Shell Spirit 2 BERMONDSEY(M)	1939	440	162	32	8½	M(A)
Toro	1961	512	171	34	10	M(A)
Ulco	1961	512	171	34	10	M(A)
Uno	1962	530	176	34	9	M(A)

J. WHARTON (SHIPPING) LTD.
Keadby

FUNNEL: *Black with black letter "W" on red diamond on broad yellow band.* HULL: *Black with blue topline and red boot-topping.*

Brendonia ...	1966	604	177	30	10	M(A)
Gladonia ...	1963	658	186	30	10	M(A)

Trent Lighterage Ltd:

Burtonia ...	1960	498	178	29	10	M(A)
Ecctonia ...	1963	658	186	30	10	M(A)
Trentonia*	1964	604	177	30	10½	M(A)

*In colours of J. W. Huelin & Co. Ltd. Jersey.

JOHN H. WHITAKER, LTD.
Hull

FUNNEL: *White with replica of houseflag on red over black over green bands.*
HULL: *Grey with red boot-topping.*

Bunkering Tanker: (Stationed at Falmouth)							
Whitonia	1965	423	182	28	10½	M(A)
ex Axel–70						

WHITEHALL SHIPPING CO. LTD.
London

FUNNEL: *Yellow.*   HULL: *Grey with red boot-topping.*

Oil/Chemical Tanker:						
Stainless Warrior	1971	1,599	285	40	12	M(A)

J. WIEGMAN SHIPPING CO. LTD.
London

FUNNEL: HULL:

Sassaby	1971	1,200dw	—	—	12¾	M(A)

J. Wharton (Shipping) Ltd.   M.V. GLADONIA   [*John G. Callis*

WILLIAMS SHIPPING CO. (FAWLEY) LTD.
Southampton

FUNNEL: HULL:

Wilclair	1935	124	91	19	7½	M(A)
ex Severn Industry–62						

B. WILLIAMS & CO. LTD.
Swansea

FUNNEL: HULL:

Gena	1930	239	130	22	8½	M(A)
ex Spray–70, Johanna–64, Friedi–52, Gruno–52						

WILSON & ISON LTD
Jersey

FUNNEL: *White.*   HULL: *Grey with white upperworks and black boot-topping.*

Nimrod	1948	399	—	—	9	M(A)

J. I. WINDSOR (SHIPPING) LTD.
Liverpool

FUNNEL: *Blue with broad white band.*   HULL: *Black.*

J. I. Windsor	1949	364	149	24	10	M(A)
ex Alcyone–70, Antares–63, Julia–54						

Irish Republic

ARKLOW SHIPPING LTD.
Arklow

FUNNEL: HULL: *Black with pink boot-topping.*

Name				Year	Tonnage	L	B	D	Engine
Arklow	...	...	...	1948	299	136	24	8½	M(A)
ex Eisbar–68, Herta II–63, Arctic–58, Banka–55									
Arklow Bay				1953	566	198	30	10½	M(A)
ex Fallowfield–71, Medusa–54									

AVOCA SHIPPING LTD.
Cork

FUNNEL: HULL:

Name				Year	Tonnage	L	B	D	Engine
Kilcrea	...	...	...	1951	389	161	25	9	M(A)
ex Fritz Raabe–70, Maria Althoff–57									

BRITISH & IRISH STEAM PACKET CO. LTD.
Dublin

FUNNEL: *White with black top and company's device in red.* HULL: *Black with green boot-topping, or blue with green boot-topping.*

Name				Year	Tonnage	L	B	D	Engine
Innisfallen	...	...	...	1968	4,849	388	59	21	M(2)
Leinster	...	...	...	1968	4,848	388	59	21	M(2)
Meath	...	...	...	1960	1,558	289	45	13	M
Munster	...	...	...	1968	4,230	361	58	21	M(2)
Wicklow	...			1971	—	325	53	14	M(A)

The company also uses chartered tonnage, notably units of the Shelbourne Shipping Co. and Dublin & Irish Sea Operators Ltd. fleets.

CELTIC COASTERS LTD.
Dublin

FUNNEL: *Black with broad band of diagonal green and white stripes.* HULL: *Grey with red boot-topping.*

Name				Year	Tonnage	L	B	D	Engine
Coastal Tankers:									
Breeda J.*	...	...	...	1952	422	165	27	9	M(A)
ex Regent Jane–67									
Celtic 1	...	...	...	1958	303	139	22	8	M(A)
ex Shell Traveller–1969									
Celtic 2	...	...	...	1956	303	139	22		M(A)
ex Shell Glassmaker–70									
Celtic 3	...	...	...	1956	301	139	22	8	M(A)
ex BP Miller–71									
Herbert D.*	...	...	...	1953	918	211	33	11	M(A)
ex Pellworm–66, Palma–61									
Mary J.	...	...	...	1955	754	196	35	10	M(A)
ex Esso Poole–68									
Rathdown	...	...	...	1965	1414	—	—	11	M(A)
ex Thorheide–70, Mikhal–67									
Rathgar	...	...	...	1959	965	217	32	11	M(A)
ex Pass of Kildrummy–70									

*Owned by Dublin Shpg Co.

British & Irish Steam Packet Co. M.V. MUNSTER

[David W. Jenkins]

CORAS IOMPAIR EIREANN
(IRISH TRANSPORT CO.)
Dublin

FUNNEL: *Red with company's winged wheel device in white between two narrow white bands.* HULL: *Orange.*

Naom Eanna	1958	483	137	29	9	M(A)
(Saint Enda)						

ARTHUR GUINNESS, SON & CO. (DUBLIN) LTD
Dublin

FUNNEL: *Red with black top.* HULL: *Blue with white line and red boot-topping.*

The Lady Grania	1952	1,152	213	36	11	M(A)
The Lady Gwendolen	1953	1,166	213	36	11	M(A)
The Lady Patricia	1962	1,187	213	38	11	M(A)

The ships sail under the British flag.

GREENORE FERRY SERVICES, LTD.
Dublin

FUNNEL: *Orange with green top separated by white band with company device.* HULL: *Grey with blue boot-topping.*

Owenbawn	1950	1,438	247	37	13	M(A)
ex Lady Sanchia—68, Alfonso—66						
Owenglas †	1970	763	257	39	12½	M(A)
Owenro	1965	598	214	32	12	M(A)

†Chartered to Coast Lines and renamed Irish Coast

HALL & TYRRELL
Arklow

FUNNEL: *Blue with black top and houseflag (white with blue "HT" monogram).* HULL: *Grey with red boot-topping.*

River Avoca	1948	384	148	25	9	M(A)
ex Stevonia—62						

IRISH SEA OPERATORS LTD.
Dublin

FUNNEL and HULL: *Trading in colours of the British & Irish Steam Packet Co.*

Mayo	1970	756	257	39	13½	M(A)
ex Hibernian Enterprise—71						
Sligo	1971	—	—	—	—	M(A)

GEORGE KEARON LTD.
Arklow

FUNNEL: *Green with orange letter "K" in white-edged green diamond with or without black top.* HULL: *Black with red boot-topping.*

Gloria				1951	446	163	25	10	M(A)
Ex Gracia									
Reginald Kearon				1957	464	164	28	9½	M(A)

MARINE TRANSPORT SERVICES LTD.
Cobh

FUNNEL: *Pale blue with "MARINE TRANSPORT SERVICES CORK" in black and red top.* HULL: *Black with red boot-topping.*

Celt				1946	139	85	20	7½	M(A)
ex Fishersvic–54, Vic 64–48									
Corpach				1945	145	85	20	7½	M(A)
ex Vic 95–50									
G. R. Velie				1958	506	178	29	9½	M(A)
ex Carnissesingel–66									
Mossville				1953	547	185	29	9½	M(A)
ex Castle Combe–60, Meteoor–54									
The Miller				1932	118	90	19	7	M(Aux)

PAT J. O'CONNOR
Dublin

FUNNEL: HULL: *Black with green boot-topping.*

Cork				1937	1,320	276	40	13	M
ex Kilkenny–71									

SEAFREIGHTS LTD.
Dublin

FUNNEL: *Yellow with black letter "S" on broad white band between narrow green bands.* HULL: *Grey with black boot-topping.*

Saskia				1952	498	168	27	9½	M(A)
ex Fivel–70									

SHELBOURNE SHIPOWNING CO.
Dublin

FUNNEL AND HULL: *Trading in colours of British & Irish Steam Packet Co. Ltd. Dublin.*

Kildare				1968	622	256	45	12½	M(A)
Tipperary				1969	622	256	44	12½	M(A)

G. Kearon Ltd.   M.V. REGINALD KEARON   [*David W. Jenkins*

JAMES TYRRELL LTD.
Arklow

FUNNEL: *Black or yellow with broad white band between two narrow green bands.*
HULL: *Black with red or green boot-topping.*

Darell	...	...	...	1970	499	148	28	11	M(A)
Marizell	...	...	...	1948	418	159	26	10	M(A)
	ex Kate–59, A. R. Rawal!–56								
Murell	...	...	...	1940	319	139	25	8	M(A)
	ex Creekdoawn–54, Goldfaun–52, Empire Estuary–46, Fiddown–43								
Shevrell	...	...	...	1954	561	200	30	10	M(A)
	ex Fernfield–72								
Valzell	...	...	...	1935	576	176	31	9½	M(A)

MICHAEL G. TYRRELL
Arklow

FUNNEL: *Green with orange letter "T" in white triangle.*   HULL: *Grey with black boot-topping.*

Avondale	...	...	...	1950	303	144	24	8	M(A)
	ex Aegir–59, Navis–56								

PILOT, LIGHTHOUSE & BUOY TENDERS

CLYDE PILOTAGE AUTHORITY
Glasgow

FUNNEL: HULL:

Pilot Tender:									
Cumbrae	...	...	...	1936	101	90	20	10	M(2)

COMMISSIONERS OF NORTHERN LIGHTHOUSES
Leith

FUNNEL: *Yellow-brown.*   HULL: *Black with white line and red boot-topping.*

Lighthouse Tenders:									
Fingal	...	...	...	...	1964	1,342	239	40	—	M(2)
Hesperus	...	...	...	...	1939	922	211	36	12	M(2)
Pharos	...	...	...	...	1955	1,712	257	40	14	M(2)
Pole Star	...	...	...	...	1961	1,328	236	40	14	M(2)

COMMISSIONERS OF IRISH LIGHTS
Dublin

FUNNEL: *Yellow.*   HULL: *Black with white line and red boot-topping.*

Lighthouse Tenders:									
Atlanta	...	...	...	1959	1,185	213	38	—	DE(2)
Granuaile	...	...	...	—	2,000	—	—	—	—
Granuaile II	...	...	1948	1,149	230	37	13½	SR(2)
ex *Granuaile–69*								
Isolda	...	...	...	1953	1,173	233	38	12½	SR(2)

CORPORATION OF TRINITY HOUSE
London

FUNNEL: *Yellow.*   HULL: *Black with white line and red boot-topping.*

Lighthouse Tenders:

Alert	1946	1,548	244	36	10	SR(2)
Argus	1948	1,918	267	40	12	SR(2)
Mermaid	1959	1,425	221	38	—	DE(2)
Ready	1947	1,920	267	40	12	SR(2)
Siren	1960	1,425	221	38	—	DE(2)
Stella	1961	1,425	221	38	—	DE(2)
Vestal	1947	1,918	268	40	12	SR(2)
Winston Churchill	1963	1,451	222	38	13½	DE(2)

Pilot Tenders:

Bembridge	1938	413	150	27	—	M(2)
Pathfinder	1954	678	175	30	—	M(2)
Patricia	1938	1,073	232	36	10	M(2)
Patrol	1961	335	139	24	—	M(2)
Pelorus	1948	443	153	28	9	M(2)
Penlee	1948	443	153	28	9	M(2)
Preceder	1961	335	139	24	—	M(2)

MERSEY DOCKS & HARBOUR COMPANY
Liverpool

FUNNEL: *Yellow with black top.*   HULL: *Black with red boot-topping.*

Pilot Tenders:

Arnet Robinson	1958	734	177	32	—	M(2)
Edmund Gardner	1953	617	177	32	—	M(2)
Sir Thomas Brocklebank	1950	675	175	32	12	M(2)

Salvage Ships and Buoy Tenders:

Salvor	1947	671	173	35	12½	SR(2)
Vigilant	1953	728	173	35	12½	SR(2)

PORT TALBOT PILOTAGE AUTHORITY
Port Talbot

FUNNEL: HULL:

Pilot Tender:

Margam Abbey	1959	117	88	20	10½	M

OIL RIG SERVICING, SUPPLY AND RESEARCH VESSELS

CARDLINE SHIPPING CO. LTD.
Lowestoft

FUNNEL: Name	Built	HULL: Tons	Length	Breadth	Speed	Engines
Research Vessels:						
Inspector	1943	347	—	—	—	M(A)
ex Hornoy–70, Grane, Adolf von Trotha						
Researcher	1950	433	—	—	—	M(A)
ex Ingoy–70						
Surveyor	1937	491	—	—	—	M(A)
ex May III–63, May–61						

OFFSHORE MARINE LTD.
(CUNARD GROUP)
London

FUNNEL:				HULL:			
Oil Rig Supply Ships:							
Arctic Shore	1969	677	177	38	12½	M(2A)
Atlantic Shore	1968	500	168	37	12	M(2A)
Bay Shore	1971	500	167	37	12	M(2A)
Cape Shore	1970	694	184	38	13½	M(2A)
East Shore	1966	669	165	38	12	M(2A)
Essex Shore	1967	499	168	37	12	M(2A)
Island Shore	1970	694	184	38	13½	M(2A)
Kent Shore	1967	664	165	38	12	M(2A)
Norfolk Shore	1967	499	168	37	12	M(2A)
North Shore	1965	677	177	38	12½	M(2A)
Nova Shore	1969	677	176	38	12½	M(2A)
Pacific Shore	1969	678	178	38	12½	M(2A)
Petrel Shore	1970	412	138	33	11	M(2A)
Polar Shore	1971	699	184	39	12	M(2A)
South Shore	1965	451	149	35	11	M(2A)
Strait Shore	1971	498	167	37	12	M(2A)
Suffolk Shore	1967	664	165	38	12	M(2A)
Tropic Shore	1969	500	167	37	12	M(2A)
West Shore	1967	696	172	39	12	M(2A)

X OCEAN SHORE   DOGGER SHORE   VIKING SHORE

OFFSHORE OIL RIG SERVICES LTD.
Great Yarmouth

FUNNEL:		HULL:				
Oil Rig Servicing Ships:						
Young Ann	1937	292	—	—	—	M(A)
ex Nettuno–69, Pursuit–68, Robrix–63						
Young Elizabeth	1953	115	—	—	—	M(A)

P. & O. OFFSHORE SERVICES LTD.
London

FUNNEL: *Yellow with black top.*   HULL:

Oil Rig Supply Ships:								
Lady Alison	...	...	...	1965	854	188	38	—	M(2A)
Lady Brigid	...	...	...	1966	677	158	38	—	M(2A)
Lady Claudine	...	...	...	1966	620	158	37	—	M(2A)
Lady Delia	...	...	...	1966	773	170	38	—	M(2A)
Lady Fiona	...	...	...	1966	773	170	38	—	M(2A)

Part of the International Offshore Services (UK) Ltd. group. Vessels of other subsidiary companies fly the Netherlands, French or Liberian flag.

SPURN SHIPPING CO. LTD.
Grimsby

FUNNEL: HULL:

Oil Rig Supply Ship:								
Spurn Haven	...	...	...	1966	247	105	26	—	M(2)
ex Lady Edwina–70								

UNITED TOWING LTD.
Hull

FUNNEL: *White with black top.*   HULL: *Black with white line and green boot-topping.*

Oil Rig Supply Ship:								
Dauntless Star	...	...	...	1948	133	96	21	—	M
ex Swiftburn, Boston Swift–57, Sunlit Waters–52								

WIMPEY MARINE LTD.
London

FUNNEL: HULL:

Oil Rig Supply Ships:							
Wimbrown One	...	...	1965	697	162	37	—	M(2)
Wimbrown Two	...	...	1965	725	162	37	—	M(2)
Brown & Root-Wimpey Ltd.							
Wimbrown Three	...	...	1966	696	162	37	—	M(2)

ZAPATA OFFSHORE SERVICES LTD
London

FUNNEL: HULL:

Oil Rig Supply Ships:							
Imperial Service	...	...	1971	689	184	39	16	M(2A)
Monarch Service	...	...	1971	—	—	—	—	M(2A)
Paramount Service	...	...	1971	692	184	39	16	M(2A)

International Offshore Services Ltd. M.V. LADY DELIA

[*M. J. Gaston*]

DREDGERS AND OTHER MAJOR HARBOUR CRAFT

BLYTH HARBOUR COMMISSIONERS
Blyth

FUNNEL: *Cream with black top.* HULL: *Black with white line.*

Name				Built	Tons	Length	Breadth	Speed	Engines
Grab Hopper Dredger:									
Cresswell ...	...		...	1959	374	136	30	—	M(A)
Trailing Suction Dredger									
Crofton	...	...	...	1963	1,062	195	42	—	DE(2A)

PORT OF BOSTON AUTHORITY
Boston, Lincs.

FUNNEL: *White with black top.* HULL: *Black with red boot-topping.*

Name				Built	Tons	Length	Breadth	Speed	Engines
Grab Hopper Dredger:									
Jean Ingelow	...	...	...	1950	149	194	25	7½	M(A)

PORT OF BRISTOL AUTHORITY
Bristol

FUNNEL: *Black with broad white band with red rectangles thereon.* HULL: *Black with red boot-topping (Except Avon, blue with City of Bristol coat-of-arms).*

Name				Built	Tons	Length	Breadth	Speed	Engines
Grab Hopper Dredgers:									
Clifton	...	...	...	1968	1,150	202	44	10½	M(2A)
Suction Hopper Dredgers:									
S.D. Severn	...	...	...	1966	1,287	212	44	—	M(2A)
Hopper Barges:									
Avon	...	...	...	1956	542	175	30	9½	M(2A)
Frome	...	...	...	1956	542	175	30	9½	M(2A)
Kingroad ...	...	...	...	1953	1,045	199	39	9½	M(2A)
Sludge Carrier:									
Glen Avon	...	...	...	1969	859	195	43	11½	M(2A)

BRITISH TRANSPORT DOCKS BOARD
London

FUNNEL: *Blue with white Bollard device.* HULL: *Black.*

Name				Built	Tons	Length	Breadth	Speed	Engines
Grab Hopper Dredgers:									
Aberavon ...	...	...	...	1969	2,156	251	50	—	M(A)
Breckland	...	...	...	1960	418	133	33	9½	M(A)
Burcom Sand	...	...	...	1954	678	170	34	9½	M(A)

BRITISH TRANSPORT DOCKS BOARD *continued*

Name				Year					
Calatria	...	...	...	1961	1,034	201	39	10	M(A)
Cave Sand	...	...	...	1968	1,080	206	41	10½	M(A)
Cherry Sand	...	...	...	1968	1,080	206	40	10	M(A)
Cressington	...	...	...	1962	1,431	213	46	12	M(A)
Ely	...	...	...	1961	1,430	228	45	9¾	M(A)
Goole Bight	...	...	...	1958	325	119	29	9	M(A)
Grassendale	...	...	...	1954	677	165	34	9	M(A)
Haile Sand	...	...	...	1963	869	157	34	9½	M(A)
Hebble Sand	...	...	...	1963	869	157	34	9½	M(A)
Kenfig	...	...	...	1954	677	165	34	9	M(A)
Lake Lothing	...	...	...	1955	659	165	34	9	M(A)
Ogmore	...	...	...	1967	609	150	35	10	M(A)
Oyster Sand	...	...	...	1966	609	149	35	10	M(A)
Redcliffe Sand	...	...	...	1964	1,424	214	45	11	M(A)
Rhymney	...	...	...	1960	710	165	35	9	M(A)
Trinity Sand	...	...	...	1961	1,252	212	45	9½	M(A)

Bucket Dredger:

Abertawe	...	...	...	1929	141	193	41	8½	SR(A)

Suction Hopper Dredgers:

Afan	...	...	...	1961	1,000	199	38	10	M(A)
Baglan	...	...	...	1966	1,889	250	48	12	DE(A)
Bleasdale	...	...	...	1962	1,029	193	40	10½	DE(A)
Clee Ness	...	...	...	1962	1,436	223	45	10	M(A)
Lavernock	...	...	...	1967	1,864	250	48	12	DE(A)
Skitter Ness	...	...	...	1964	1,577	230	45	11	DE(A)

CLYDE PORT AUTHORITY
Glasgow

FUNNEL: *Yellow or black.* HULL: *Grey with red boot-topping.*

Bucket Dredgers:

Blythswood	...	...	...	1963	786	210	43	—	M(2A)
Cessnock	...	...	...	1955	723	196	41	7	SR(A)
Elderslie	...	...	...	1924	782	189	37	8	SR(2A)
Sir William H. Raeburn		...	...	1928	253	128	27	7½	SR(2A)

Grab Hopper Dredger:

Lennox II	...	...	...	1954	795	192	38	10½	SR(2A)

Also the Hopper Barges Nos. 1, 3, 10 and 25-28, of 850-1,000 g.r.t.

CONOLEY & CO. LTD.
Falmouth

FUNNEL: HULL:

Dredger:

Rosslyn	...	...	...	1912	702	196	41	7½	SR

COSTAIN BLANKEVOORT (U.K.) DREDGING CO. LTD.
London

FUNNEL: *Blue with blue letter "C" on white panel.* HULL: *Black.*

Trailing Suction Hopper Dredgers:

Tees Bay	...	...	...	1966	2,941	310	54	12	M(2A)

COSTAIN BLANKEVOORT (U.K.) DREDGING CO. LTD. *continued*

Hopper Barges:								
Thames Bay	...	...	...	1967	605	177	31	8	M(2A)
Tyne Bay ...	...	...	...	1967	606	177	31	8	M(2A)

Sand Suction Dredger:							
Eric Cooper			1965	553	157	34	—	M(A)

D. COOK, LTD.
Hull

FUNNEL: *Red with black top.*   HULL: *Black with red boot-topping.*

Grab Hopper Dredger:							
Foremost 50	...	...	...	1937	380	142	30	8½	SR(A)

DOVER HARBOUR BOARD
Dover

FUNNEL: HULL: *Black.*

Grab Hopper Dredger:						
Admiral Day	...	...	1971	350	—	—	—	M(A)

FORTH PORTS AUTHORITY
Leith

FUNNEL: *Black.*   HULL: *Black.*

Suction Hopper Dredger:							
Abbotsgrange	...	...	...	1967	1,864	250	48	12	M(2A)

IPSWICH DOCK COMMISSION
Ipswich

FUNNEL: *Yellow with black top.*   HULL: *Black.*

Grab Hopper Dredger:							
Samuel Armstrong	...	...	1956	364	136	30	10	M(A)

ISLE OF MAN HARBOUR BOARD
Douglas, I.O.M.

FUNNEL: HULL:

Grab Hopper Dredger:							
Mannin	...	...	...	...	1936	123	100	23	—	SR(A)

JAMES CONTRACTING & SHIPPING CO. LTD.
Southampton

FUNNEL: *White with diagonal yellow over blue panel.* HULL: *Black or grey.*

Suction Hopper Dredgers:							
Foremost Prince	...	...	1933	849	195	38	9	SR(2)
The Solent			1958	2,105	300	44	—	M(2A)
ex H.A.M. 303								
Hopper Barges:							
Foremost 101	...	...	...	1939	871	194	33	8½	M(A)
Foremost 102	...	...	...	1940	871	194	33	8½	M(A)
W. D. Itchen	...	...	...	1970	1,193	230	43	9½	M(A)
W. D. Test	...	...	...	1970	1,193	230	43	9½	M(A)
Launched as **Foremost Test**								

MANCHESTER SHIP CANAL CO. LTD.
Manchester

FUNNEL: *Black with two black bands.* HULL: *Black.*

Bucket Dredger:							
Gowy	...	...	...	1924	415	160	36	—	SR(A)
Grab Hopper Dredgers:							
Grab Hopper No. 1	...	...	1949	479	150	32	—	M(A)
Grab Hopper No. 2	...	...	1959	129	103	25	—	M(2A)

MERSEY DOCKS & HARBOUR COMPANY
Liverpool, Birkenhead, etc.

FUNNEL: *Yellow with black top.* HULL: *Dark grey with red boot-topping.*

Grab Hopper Dredgers:							
Mersey Compass	...	...	1961	2,083	275	48	—	DE(2A)
Mersey No. 14	...	...	1949	459	145	32	10	DE(2A)
Mersey No. 26	...	...	1948	1,363	238	41	11	DE(2A)
Mersey No. 27	...	...	1949	1,363	238	41	11	DE(2A)
Mersey No. 40	...	...	1957	1,968	263	48	11½	M(2A)
Mersey No. 41	...	...	1957	1,364	238	41	11	M(2A)
Hopper Barge:							
Mersey No. 42	...	...	1957	637	167	36	10	M(A)

MINISTRY OF THE ENVIRONMENT
Portsmouth, Plymouth, etc.

FUNNEL: HULL:

Bucket Dredgers:							
St. Abbs	...	...	...	1946	512	154	36	—	SR(A)
ex Empire Champion—47								
St. Ives (W.2)	...	...	1946	938	195	40	—	SR(A)
ex Empire Mammoth—46								
Grab Hopper Dredgers:							
St. Giles (W.6)	...	...	1951	619	—	—	—	SR(2A)
St. Martin (W.8)	...	...	1951	389	—	—	—	SR(2A)
Servitor (W.9)	...	...	1935	572	—	—	—	—

MINISTRY OF THE ENVIRONMENT *continued*

Hopper Barges:

St. Bees (W.36)	1968	1,162	—	—	—	M(A)
W.29	1945	683	167	33	—	SR(2A)
ex *Empire Moorland–48*						
W.30	1946	683	167	33	—	SR(2A)
ex *Empire Marshland–47*						
W.31	1944	683	167	33	—	SR(2A)
ex *Empire Dockland–48*						
W.32	1946	683	167	33	—	SR(2A)
ex *Empire Woodland–48*						
W.34	1947	273	—	—	—	—

PORT OF LONDON AUTHORITY
London

FUNNEL: *Yellow.* HULL: *Black.*

Grab Hopper Dredgers:

Gallions Reach	1936	795	178	34	10½	SR(A)
Long Reach	1961	1,972	264	47	11½	SR(2A)

Hopper Barges:

Asa Binns	1964	847	205	35	—	M(2A)
Cyril Kirkpatrick	1964	847	205	35	—	M(2A)

POOLE HARBOUR COMMISSIONERS
Poole

FUNNEL: HULL:

Hopper Dredger:

C. H. Horn	1968	159	85	29	6½	M(A)

COUNTY BOROUGH OF PRESTON
Preston

FUNNEL: *Black with County Borough coat-of-arms.* HULL: *Black.*

Hopper Dredgers:

Astland	1948	1,287	210	40	8½	SR(A)
Calder	1949	618	173	32	8½	SR(A)
Ribble	1948	1,287	210	40	8½	SR(A)
Savick	1949	618	173	32	8½	SR(A)

BOROUGH OF RAMSGATE
Ramsgate

FUNNEL: HULL:

Grab Hopper Dredger:

Ramsgate	1962	168	102	26	—	M(A)

SCARBOROUGH CORPORATION
Scarborough

FUNNEL: *Yellow.* HULL: *Black with red boot-topping.*

Grab Hopper Dredger:								
Skarthi	1952	112	84	23	7	M(A)

SHOREHAM PORT AUTHORITY
Shoreham

FUNNEL: *Black.* HULL: *Black.*

Bucket Dredger:								
Adur	1954	199	148	25	6	SR(A)

SEAHAM HARBOUR DOCK CO. LTD.
Seaham Harbour

FUNNEL: HULL: *Black.*

Grab Hopper Dredger:								
Wynyard ... ... ex *Ramsgate–62*	1936	220	109	27	7½	SR(A)

PORT OF TYNE AUTHORITY
Newcastle

FUNNEL: HULL:

Grab Hopper Dredger:								
Hedwin	1969	666	157	39	—	M(A)
Hopper Barges:								
Bobby Shaftoe	1955	561	158	33	10¾	M(A)
Hexhamshire Lass	1955	561	158	33	10½	M(A)

WESTMINSTER DREDGING CO. LTD.
London

FUNNEL: HULL: *Black or grey.*

Trailing Suction Hopper Dredgers:								
Prins van Nederlanden ...	—	10,586	468	72	16	M(2A)
W. D. Fairway	1941	1,299	227	39	—	M(2A)
W. D. Hoyle	1967	1,223	233	39	11	M(2A)
W. D. Seaway	1963	4,712	360	60	—	M(2A)
W. D. Tideway	1966	4,030	332	55	—	M(2A)
W. D. Waterway	1941	1,424	249	39	—	M(2A)
ex *W.D. 52–62, Marga*							

WESTMINSTER DREDGING CO. LTD. *continued*

Bucket Dredger:						
Stewart Clan	1936	398	148	34	—	—

Hopper Dredgers:						
Resolution	1971	4,900	—	—	—	M(2A)
W. D. Gateway	1969	8,168	423	64	16	M(2A)
W. D. Mersey	1960	2,851	301	53	—	M(2A)
W. D. Seven Seas	1959	2,034	291	44	—	M(2A)
W. D. Thames	1939	1,887	258	43	—	M(2A)
ex Batavus–65						

Hopper Barges:						
Barrow Deep	1926	911	190	39	—	M(2A)
Black Deep	1925	914	190	39	—	M(2A)
Knock Deep	1927	912	190	39	—	M(2A)
Lune Deep	1936	895	190	40	—	M(2A)
Middle Deep	1927	912	190	39	—	M(2A)
South Deep	1936	917	197	40	—	M(2A)
W. D. Clyde	1963	1,078	214	38	—	M(A)
W. D. Delta	1920	400	164	31	—	M(2A)
ex M.S.C. Delta–54, G.W.C. No. 12						
W. D. Gamma	1920	456	164	31	—	M(2A)
ex M.S.C. Gamma–54, G.W.C. No. 11						
W. D. Hilbre	1967	1,112	214	39	11	M(2A)
W. D. Tyne	1963	1,079	214	38	11	M(2A)

Working in the Thames and Mersey and on overseas contracts.

TEES & HARTLEPOOLS PORT AUTHORITY
Middlesbrough

FUNNEL: HULL:

Hopper Dredger:						
Heortnesse	1959	604	156	43	—	M(2A)

Suction Hopper Dredger:						
T.C.C. Dredger No. 1	1951	1,206	220	41	—	SR(2A)

Also the 650-750 g.r.t. Hopper Barges Nos. 3, 5 and 6.

WORKINGTON HARBOUR & DOCK BOARD
Workington

FUNNEL: *Black.*   HULL: *Black.*

Bucket Dredgers:						
Cocur	1949	588	175	38	—	SR(A)

Hopper Barges:						
Moss Bay	1901	434	172	27	7	SR(A)
Old Side	1908	436	172	27	7	SR(A)
ex Scudhill						

Irish Republic

CORK HARBOUR COMMISSIONERS
Cork

FUNNEL: *White with black top.*   HULL: *Black.*

Hopper Dredger:									
Grabwell ...	...	...	...	1935	251	115	28	—	SR(A)

LIMERICK HARBOUR COMMISSIONERS
Limerick

FUNNEL: HULL:

Grab and Suction Hopper Dredger:								
Curraghgour II ...	...	...	1959	459	143	32	8	M(A)

COMMISSIONER OF PUBLIC WORKS IN IRELAND
Dublin

FUNNEL: HULL:

Bucket Hopper Dredger:									
Sisyphus ...	...	...	...	1905	284	119	26	—	SR(A)

TUGS

ABERDEEN HARBOUR BOARD
Aberdeen

FUNNEL: *Black with letters "A H B" on broad yellow band between two narrow red bands.* HULL: *Black with red boot-topping.*

AREA OF OPERATIONS: *Aberdeen Harbour.*

Name				Built	Tons Gross	Horse Power	Engine
Sea Griffon	...	...	...	1961	117	800 (B)	M
Sea Trojan	...	...	...	1961	117	800 (B)	M

ALEXANDRA TOWING CO. LTD.
Liverpool

FUNNEL: *Yellow with black top separated by broad white band over narrow black ring.* HULL: *Black with white topline and red boot-topping.*

AREAS OF OPERATION: *Liverpool and River Mersey; Southampton and the Solent; Swansea, Port Talbot and the Bristol Channel.*

Name				Built	Tons Gross	Horse Power	Engine
Alexandra	...	...	...	1963	161	940 (B)	M
Alfred	...	...	...	1971	278	2,400 (B)	M
Brockenhurst	...	...	...	1964	174	1,200 (B)	M
Brocklebank	...	...	...	1965	172	1,200 (B)	M
Cambrian	...	...	...	1960	163	890 (B)	M
Canning	...	...	...	1954	200	950 (I)	SR
Crosby	...	...	...	1971	260	2,400 (B)	M/K/FF
Egerton	...	...	...	1965	142	1,200 (B)	M
Gower	...	...	...	1961	152	960 (B)	M
Herculaneum	...	...	...	1962	161	940 (B)	M/K
Langton	...	...	...	1964	172	1,200 (B)	M
Margam	...	...	...	1971	280	2,190 (B)	M/K/FF
Mumbles	...	...	...	1969	291	2,100 (B)	M/K
Nelson	...	...	...	1966	173	1,200 (B)	M
North Beach	...	...	...	1956	220	1,050 (I)	SR
North Buoy	...	...	...	1959	219	1,000 (I)	SR
North End	...	...	...	1957	215	1,000 (I)	SR
North Isle	...	...	...	1959	200	1,350 (B)	M
North Light	...	...	...	1956	206	1,050 (I)	SR
North Loch	...	...	...	1959	200	1,350 (B)	M
North Quay	...	...	...	1956	219	1,050 (I)	SR
North Rock	...	...	...	1956	206	1,050 (I)	SR
North Wall	...	...	...	1959	219	1,050 (I)	SR
Ower	...	...	...	1944	55	450 (B)	M
ex President Breward–66, Tid–78							
Romsey	...	...	...	1964	174	1,200 (B)	M
Talbot	...	...	...	1961	153	960 (B)	M
Trafalgar	...	...	...	1966	174	1,200 (B)	M
Ventnor	...	...	...	1965	173	1,200 (B)	M
Wallasey	...	...	...	1954	200	950 (I)	SR
Waterloo	...	...	...	1954	200	850 (I)	SR

J. H. Lamey, Ltd.:

Name				Built	Tons Gross	Horse Power	Engine
Coburg	...	...	...	1967	220	1,400 (B)	M
ex Alfred Lamey–70							
Hornby	...	...	...	1963	200	1,350 (B)	M
ex J. H. Lamey–70							
Huskisson	...	...	...	1968	225	1,700 (B)	M
ex James Lamey–70							

ALEXANDRA TOWING CO. LTD. *continued*

Salthouse	1966	215	1,400 (B)	M
ex B. C. Lamey–70				
Wapping	1959	166	1,000 (B)	M
Liverpool Screw Towing Co. Ltd:				
Canada	1960	165	1,088 (B)	M
ex Pea Cock–70				
Collingwood	1958	193	1,170 (B)	M
ex Heath Cock–70				
Formby	1960	159	1,066 (B)	M
ex Weather Cock–70				
Gladstone	1960	159	1,080 (B)	M
ex Flying Cock–70				
Morpeth	1958	193	1,170 (B)	M
ex West Cock–70				

Britannia Steam Towing Co: (Black funnel with silver band).

Trover	1945	54	~~220~~ 450 (I)	~~SR~~ M
ex Sunnyside, –Tid				

ARDROSSAN HARBOUR CO. LTD.
Ardrossan

FUNNEL: *Black with houseflag on broad white band.*   HULL: *Black with white line and red boot-topping.*

AREA OF OPERATION: *Ardrossan.*

Ardmeil	1953	300	1,750 (B)	M
ex Cruiser–69				

Alexandra Towing Co.   M.T. BROCKENHURST   [*R. J. Weeks*

F. A. ASHMEAD & SONS, LTD.
Bristol

FUNNEL: *Black with broad red band between two narrow white bands.* HULL: *Black with white line.*

AREA OF OPERATIONS: *Bristol, Avonmouth and Bristol Channel (Lighterage).*

Judith A.	...	...	—	—	—	M	
ex Conroy–63							
Peter Leigh ...	...	...	1936	49	300 (B)	M	
ex John King–70							
Robert A.	...	...	1934	32	—	M	
ex Volunteer–59							
Thelm Leigh ...	...	...	1897	64	—	M rbt fm SR	
ex Resolute–70							

ASSOCIATED PORTLAND CEMENT MANUFACTURERS LTD.
London

FUNNEL: *Black with white band bordered by blue and yellow bands with "Blue" on the upper yellow band and "Circle" on the lower.* HULL: *Black with two white lines and red boot-topping.*

AREA OF OPERATION: *River Thames and Medway (Company's Lighterage).*

Cemenco	1948	116	720 (B)	M
Cullamix	1938	96	650 (B)	M
Impermo	1935	38	200 (B)	M
ex Benbow–60, Temeritie				
Sandtex	1950	92	605 (B)	M
ex Silverdial–70				

BANTRY BAY TOWING CO. LTD.
Cobh

See Wm. Cory Group

C. W. BECKETT, LTD.
London

FUNNEL: *Yellow with red letters "C W B".* HULL: *Black.*

AREA OF OPERATION: *River Thames (Lighterage).*

Bess...	1944	55	240 (B)	M
ex Industrious–65, Tanac 66				

BELFAST HARBOUR COMMISSIONERS
Belfast

FUNNEL: *Yellow with black top.* HULL: *Black with red boot-topping.*
AREA OF OPERATION: *Belfast.*

Ada Dorothy	...	...	...	1971	54	337 (B)	M
David Andrews	...	...	...	1971	50	337 (B)	M
Sir Kenneth	...	...	...	1958	75	330 (B)	M
Sir Milne	...	...	...	1945	54	220 (I)	SR
ex Tid 152							
Somerton	...	...	...	1945	54	220 (I)	SR
ex Tid 156							

BLYTH HARBOUR COMMISSIONERS
Blyth

FUNNEL: *Cream with black top.* HULL: *Black with white line.*
AREA OF OPERATIONS: *Blyth.*

Horton	...	...	...	1968	—	240 (B)	MK

Bantry Bay Towing Co.   M.T. BRANDON BAY   [*D. Lynch*

BLYTH TUG CO. LTD.
Blyth

FUNNEL: *Yellow with blue Maltese cross.*   HULL: *Black.*
AREA OF OPERATIONS: *Blyth.*

Hillsider	1924	177	800 (I)	SR
ex *Headman–62*				
Maximus	1956	141	750 (B)	M/K

PORT OF BOSTON AUTHORITY
Boston, Lincs.

FUNNEL: *White with black top.*   HULL: *Black with red boot-topping.*
AREA OF OPERATIONS: *Boston, Lincs.*

Bostonian	1967	50	528 (B)	M

BOSTON DEEP SEA FISHERIES LTD.
Lowestoft

FUNNEL: *(None).*   HULL: *Black with white line and red boot-topping.*
AREA OF OPERATION: *Lowestoft.*

Columbus	1954	35	350 (B)	M
ex *Wilhelmina 8*				
Corlea	1933	31	100 (B)	M

BRAITHWAITE & DEAN, LTD.
London

FUNNEL: *White with narrow black top.*   HULL: *Black.*
AREA OF OPERATION: *River Thames (Lighterage).*

Charlock	1962	42	385 (B)	M

CHAS. BRAND, LTD.
Belfast

FUNNEL: *Black.*   HULL: *Black with red boot-topping.*
AREA OF OPERATION: *Belfast (Contract work).*

Lavinia	1928	300	900 (I)	SR
ex *Sloyne–66*				
Lilias	1928	260	950 (I)	SR
ex *James Lamey–66, Flying Eagle–59*				

BRISTOL DOCKS AUTHORITY
Bristol

FUNNEL: *Black with band of red squares superimposed on broader white band.*
HULL: *Black with red boot-topping.*

AREA OF OPERATION: *Bristol and Avonmouth.*

Cabot	...	...	...	...	1952	98	—	M

BRITISH RAILWAYS BOARD
London

FUNNEL: *None.* HULL: *Dark blue with British Rail "Twin-Arrow" device on bridge-house.*

AREA OF OPERATION: *Newhaven, Sussex.*

Meeching	...	...	...	1960	160	1,040 (B)	M

BRITISH TRANSPORT DOCKS BOARD
London

FUNNEL: *Blue, with or without black top, with white bollard device.* HULL: *Black.*

AREA OF OPERATION: *Barrow-in-Furness and Fleetwood, Hull, Newport.*

Landy II	...	...	...	...	1949	66	204 (B)	M(2)
Llanwern	...	...	...	...	1960	190	1,200 (B)	DE(2)
Newport	...	...	...	...	1955	139	700 (B)	M
Rampside	...	...	...	...	1941	260	1,000 (I)	SR
ex Central No. 3–57, Empire Fir–46								
Roa	...	...	...	...	1944	232	900 (I)	SR
ex Central No. 4–57, Empire Polly–46								
St. Woolas	...	...	...	...	1960	160	1,200 (B)	M(2)
Wyke	...	...	...	...	1956	62	480 (B)	M

BRITISH WATERWAYS BOARD
Gloucester and Goole

FUNNEL: HULL: *Black.*

AREAS OF OPERATION: *River Severn and Goole (Aire & Calder Canal, etc.)*

Severn Fleet:							
Primrose	...	...	...	1906	52	180 (I)	SR
Severn Active	...	...	...	1904	—	204 (B)	M
Speedwell	...	...	...	1968	50	330 (B)	M
Stanegarth	...	...	...	1910	47	—	M
Goole Fleet:							
Allerton Bywater	...	...	1960	53	135 (B)	M
Brodsworth	...	...	...	1960	53	135 (B)	M
Freight Pioneer	...	...	...	1970	—	300 (B)	M/Pusher
Freight Trader	...	...	...	1971	—	300 (B)	M/Pusher
Hatfield	...	...	...	1959	53	135 (B)	M
Water Haigh	...	...	...	1960	53	135 (B)	M
West Riding	...	...	...	1958	53	135 (B)	M

British Waterways   M.T. SPEEDWELL   [*P. C. White*

T. R. BROWN & SONS LTD.
Bristol

FUNNEL: *Black with broad red band between two narrow white bands.*   HULL: *Black with white line.*

AREA OF OPERATION: *Avonmouth and Bristol (Lighterage).*

Ernest Brown	...	...	...	1944	54	220 (B)	M
ex Tid 95							

CAWOOD HARGREAVES, LTD.
Hull

FUNNEL: *(None).*   HULL: *Black.*

AREAS OF OPERATION: *Inland Rivers and Canals from Hull and Goole.*

CH 106	...	...	...	...	1967	60	150 (B)	M/Pusher
CH 107	...	...	...	...	1967	60	150 (B)	M/Pusher
CH 108	...	...	...	...	1967	60	150 (B)	M/Pusher
CH 109	...	...	...	...	1967	60	150 (B)	M/Pusher

CHRISTIANIE & NEILSON, LTD.
London

FUNNEL: *Yellow with black top and with blue "CN" monogram in white disc.*
HULL: *Black.*
AREA OF OPERATION: *Contract work.*

Chrianie 1954					54	220 (I)	SR
ex Tid 107							

CLEMENTS, TOUGH LTD.
London

FUNNEL: *Yellow with red band and monogram.* HULL: *Black with white line and red boot-topping.*
AREA OF OPERATION: *River Thames (Lighterage).*

Fenland 1929					38	400 (B)	M rbt fm SR
ex Seaby							
Ham 1925					44	240 (B)	M rbt fm SR
Sheen 1925					52	300 (B)	M rbt fm SR

CLYDE SHIPPING CO. LTD.
Glasgow

FUNNEL: *Black.* HULL: *Black with broad ochre band having dummy black ports with a white line above.*
AREA OF OPERATION: *River Clyde and Coastal Towage.*

Flying Demon 1964				131	1,000 (B)	M	
Flying Dipper 1958				274	1,200 (B)	M	
Flying Duck 1956				176	1,040 (B)	M	
Flying Falcon 1967				213	1,470 (B)	M/K	
Flying Foam 1962				184	1,350 (B)	M	
Flying Mist 1962				190	1,350 (B)	M	
Flying Scout 1970				290	2,800 (B)	M/K	
Flying Spray 1962				150	1,350 (B)	M	
Flying Witch 1960				115	1,060 (B)	M	

COLNE FISHING CO. LTD.
Lowestoft

FUNNEL: *Blue with black top.* HULL: *Black.*
AREA OF OPERATION: *Lowestoft.*

Mardyke 1957					37	302 (B)	M
ex John Henry–60							

Christianie & Neilson Ltd.   M.T. CHRIANIE   [*M. J. Gaston*

Clements Tough Ltd.   M. T. HAM   [*M. J. Gaston*

FUNNEL: *Black with black diamond on broad white band.* HULL: *Black with white or silver band and red boot-topping.*

AREA OF OPERATIONS: *As below.*

Bantry Bay Towing Co. Ltd. (Bantry Bay and Southern Ireland Coastal):

Name				Year	Tons	Power	Type
Bantry Bay*	...	...	...	1968	299	2,500 (B)	M/FF
Brandon Bay*	...	...	...	1968	299	2,500 (B)	M/FF
Dingle Bay*	...	...	...	1968	299	2,500 (B)	M/FF
Tralee Bay*	...	...	...	1968	299	2,500 (B)	M/FF

Cory Ship Towage Ltd. (Avonmouth, Newport, Cardiff, Barry and Milford Haven):

Name				Year	Tons	Power	Type
Anglegarth	...	...	...	1960	306	1,300 (B)	M/SAL
Avongarth	...	...	...	1960	156	960 (B)	M
Bargarth ...	...	...	...	1966	161	850 (B)	M/K
Butegarth	...	...	...	1966	161	850 (B)	M/K
Dalegarth ...	...	...	...	1960	306	1,300 (B)	M/SAL
Danegarth	...	...	...	1966	161	850 (B)	M/K
Dunheron ...	...	...	...	1955	132	882 (B)	M
ex Golden Cross—68							
Dunosprey	...	...	...	1967	185	1,380 (B)	M
Falgarth ...	...	...	...	1958	102	500 (B)	M/K
ex Cleddia—62							
Glengarth	...	...	...	1970	292	2,460 (B)	M/K
Graygarth	...	...	...	1970	291	2,460 (B)	M/FF/K
Greengarth	...	...	...	1970	291	2,460 (B)	M/FF/K
Gwentgarth	...	...	...	1962	186	1,380 (B)	M
ex Dunsnipe—71							
Lowgarth	...	...	...	1965	155	850 (B)	M/K
Pengarth ...	...	...	...	1962	160	1,080 (B)	M
Plumgarth	...	...	...	1960	156	850 (B)	M
Polgarth ...	...	...	...	1962	160	1,080 (B)	M
Ramsgarth	...	...	...	1964	306	1,300 (B)	M/K
Rathgarth	...	...	...	1965	306	1,300 (B)	M/K
Reagarth ...	...	...	...	1964	306	1,300 (B)	M/K
Stackgarth	...	...	...	1959	306	1,300 (B)	M/K
Thorngarth	...	...	...	1959	306	1,300 (B)	M/K
Uskgarth ...	...	...	...	1966	161	850 (B)	M/K
Westgarth	...	...	...	1962	190	1,320 (B)	M
ex Duncurlew—71							

Cory Ship Towage (Clyde) Ltd. (Clyde and Coastal Towage):

Name				Year	Tons	Power	Type
Brigadier ...	...	...	...	1961	223	1,326 (I)	M
Campaigner	...	...	...	1957	248	1,384 (I)	M
Chieftain ...	...	...	...	1968	200	1,650 (I)	M/K
Strongbow	...	...	...	1960	225	1,326 (I)	M
Thunderer	...	...	...	1958	208	1,040 (B)	M
Vanguard ...	...	...	...	1964	224	1,020 (B)	M
Warrior ...	...	...	...	1970	300	2,400 (B)	M/K
Wrestler ...	...	...	...	1957	248	1,056 (B)	M

Cory Ship Towage (N.I.) Ltd. (Belfast, Cobh, and Coastal Towage):

Name				Year	Tons	Power	Type
Carrickfergus	...	...	...	1958	161	960 (B)	M
Cashel ...	...	...	...	1959	207	1,260 (B)	M
Clandeboye	...	...	...	1967	167	1,260 (B)	M/K/F
Clonmel ...	...	...	...	1959	207	1,260 (B)	M/K/F
Coleraine ...	...	...	...	1970	212	1,260 (B)	M
Craigdarragh	...	...	...	1966	169	1,260 (B)	M
Cultra ...	...	...	...	1962	202	1,260 (B)	M

Cory Lighterage Ltd. (River Thames (Lighterage)):

Name				Year	Tons	Power	Type
Mercedes II	...	...	...	1951	92	605 (B)	M
ex Silverbeam—71							
Recruit	...	...	...	1952	91	670 (B)	M
Redoubt ...	...	...	...	1916	71	440 (B)	M rbt fm SR
Regard ...	...	...	...	1958	69	403 (B)	M
Relentless	...	...	...	1943	61	450 (B)	M

CORY GROUP OF COMPANIES *continued*

Revenge	1948	61	528 (B)	M
Swiftstone	1952	91	670 (B)	M
Touchstone	1962	75	528 (B)	M

Mercantile Lighterage Ltd. (River Thames (Lighterage)) :

Hawkstone	1948	61	450 (B)	M
Hurricane	1938	90	660 (B)	M
Mersina	1955	79	670 (B)	M
ex Repulse				

See also Smith Cory International Port Towage Ltd.

W. S. CROUCH & SONS, LTD.
Greenhithe

FUNNEL: *Buff with red, white and blue houseflag.* HULL: *Black.*

AREA OF OPERATION: *River Thames (Lighterage).*

Lads Spearing	1936	—	375 (B)	M
ex Vange–71				

W. R. CUNIS, LTD.
London

FUNNEL: *White with black top and broad red band separated by narrow white band.* HULL: *Black with white line.*

AREA OF OPERATION: *River Thames (Lighterage).*

William Ryan	1908	72	530 (B)	M rbt fm SR
ex Toro				
Tom Jay	1945	67	408 (B)	M

DARLING BROS. LTD.
London

FUNNEL: *White with green triangle.* HULL:

AREA OF OPERATION: *River Thames (Lighterage).*

Arthur Darling	1946	50	275 (B)	M
ex John Hawkins–69				

JOHN DEHEER LTD.
Hull

FUNNEL: *Red with black top and black star.* HULL: *Black.*

AREA OF OPERATION: *Hull and River Humber (Lighterage).*

Ian	1907	67	—	SR
ex Kieve–				

J. DINWOODIE
Granton

FUNNEL: *Black.*   HULL: *Black.*

AREA OF OPERATION: *Granton.*

Inchkeith ...	...	...	...	1939	40	—	M
Inchmickry	...	...	...	1939	46	—	M

DOVER HARBOUR BOARD
Dover

FUNNEL: *(None).*   HULL: *Black with white line and green boot-topping.*

AREA OF OPERATION: *Dover and English Channel.*

Diligent ...	...	...	...	1957	161	1,040 (B)	M
Dominant	...	...	...	1958	161	1,040 (B)	M

DUNDEE HARBOUR TRUST
Dundee

FUNNEL: *Yellow with narrow black top.*   HULL: *Black with yellow line and red boot-topping.*

AREA OF OPERATION: *Dundee.*

Castlecraig ...	...	...	1951	139	660 (B)	M
ex Walcheren VIII						
Harecraig II ...	...	...	1951	261	1,180 (B)	M
ex Flying Buzzard						

ERITH & DARTFORD LIGHTERAGE CO. LTD.
Erith

FUNNEL: HULL:

AREA OF OPERATIONS:

Caroline ...	...	...	...	1937	50	340 (B)	M rbt fm SR
ex General V, Isleworth Lion						

F. T. EVERARD & SONS, LTD
Greenhithe

FUNNEL: *Black with houseflag.*   HULL: *Black with two white lines.*

AREA OF OPERATION: *River Thames (Lighterage).*

P. B. Everard ...	...	...	1951	74	450 (B)	M
ex Margaret Locket–70						
R. A. Everard ...	...	...	1943	87	760 (B)	M
ex Pinklake						
S. A. Everard ...	...	...	1939	124	800 (B)	M

FALMOUTH TOWAGE CO. LTD.
Falmouth

FUNNEL: *Black with broad white band.* HULL: *Black over green with white line and red boot-topping.*

AREA OF OPERATION: *Falmouth and Coastal towage.*

St. Agnes	1935	259	1,211 (I)	M
ex *Warrior–68*				
St. Denys	1929	174	790 (I)	SR
ex *Northgate Scot–59*				
St. Eval	1930	196	660 (B)	M
ex *Chieftain–67*				
St. Just	1957	62	—	M
ex *Lalla Rookh II–63*				
St. Levan	1942	160	700 (I)	SR
ex *Codicote Scot–59, Bruno Dreyer–51*				
St. Mawes	1951	346	800 (I)	SR
ex *Arusha–59*				
St. Merryn	1945	233	1,000 (I)	SR
ex *Rockpigeon*				

Falmouth Towage Co.   S.T. ST MERRYN   [*J. Clarkson*

FLEETWOOD FISHING VESSELS OWNERS ASSOCIATION
Fleetwood

FUNNEL: HULL:
AREA OF OPERATION: *Fleetwood Fish Docks.*

Finch 1956					58	310 (B)	M
ex Boys White–69, Falconbrook–67							

FORTH PORTS AUTHORITY
Leith

FUNNEL: *Black.*   HULL: *Black with white lines and red boot-topping.*
AREA OF OPERATION: *Leith and Firth of Forth.*

Gunnet ...	...	...	...	1967	143	1,200 (B)	M(2)/VS
Inchcolm ...	...	...	...	1967	143	1,200 (B)	M(2)/VS
Martello ...	...	...	...	1958	68	440 (B)	M/K

FOWEY HARBOUR COMMISSIONERS
Fowey

FUNNEL: *Yellow with black top.*   HULL: *Black over green with red boot-topping.*
AREA OF OPERATION: *Fowey.*

Cannis				1953	91	600 (B)	M
ex Enticette–65							
Gribbin Head				1955	132	882 (I)	M
ex Ingleby Cross–68							

FRANCE, FENWICK TYNE & WEAR CO. LTD.
Sunderland

FUNNEL: *Light blue with black top separated by broad band of blue and white diagonal stripes with a blue anchor superimposed.* HULL: *Black with yellow lines and green boot-topping.*

AREA OF OPERATION: *Sunderland and River Wear. (The company's tugs also work in Tyne Tugs colours on the River Tyne).*

Cornhill ...	...	...	...	1943	176	700 (B)	M
Dunelm ...	...	...	...	1964	150	—	M
Marsden ...	...	...	...	1956	119	1,086 (B)	M
Prestwick ...	...	...	...	1955	119	1,086 (B)	M
Whitburn ...	...	...	...	1943	176	700 (B)	M
ex Kronos–64							

GASELEE & KNIGHT LTD.
London

FUNNEL: *Black with two white bands each bordered by two narrow red bands.*
HULL: *Black with white line and red boot-topping.*

AREA OF OPERATION: *River Thames (Lighterage).*

Agama	1937	84	500 (B)	M rbt fm SR
Mamba	1935	66	390 (B)	M rbt fm SR
Naja	1936	62	300 (B)	M rbt fm SR
ex Servis				

Tugs owned by J. P. Knight Ltd., also work under the management of the company.

GASELEE (FELIXSTOWE) LTD.
Felixstowe

FUNNEL: *Yellow with three narrow red bands and Dick & Page houseflag super-imposed.* HULL: *Black with white line and red boot-topping.*

AREA OF OPERATION: *Felixstowe, Harwich, etc.*

Sauria	1968	165	—	M/FF

GILYOTT & SCOTT, LTD.
Hull

FUNNEL: *Yellow with black letter "G".* HULL: *Black.*

AREA OF OPERATION: *River Humber, etc. (Lighterage).*

Gillian Knight	1963	32	—	M
Hippo D.	1931	45	220 (B)	M rbt fm SR
ex Lion H.				

GRANGEMOUTH & FORTH TOWING
CO. LTD.
Grangemouth

FUNNEL: *Yellow with black top.* HULL: *Black with red boot-topping.*

AREA OF OPERATIONS: *Grangemouth and Methil.*

Dalgrain	1963	140	840 (B)	M
Dundas	1931	150	1,000 (I)	SR
ex Stronghold–49				
Forth	1967	184	1,140 (B)	M/K
Kerse	1923	214	800 (I)	SR
Zetland	1961	138	840 (B)	M/K

GREAT YARMOUTH PORT AND HAVEN COMMISSIONERS
Great Yarmouth

FUNNEL: *Yellow with black top.*   HULL: *Black with white line.*
AREA OF OPERATION: *Great Yarmouth.*

Hector Reed	...	...	...	1966	65	590 (B)	M

GRAVESEND TOWING SERVICES
Gravesend

FUNNEL: *Green with broad white band.*   HULL: *Black.*
AREA OF OPERATION: *River Thames (Lighterage).*

General IV	...	...	...	1936	50	390 (B)	M
Pullette	...	...	...	1925	33	—	M
ex Thorec							

GREENHITHE LIGHTERAGE CO. LTD.
Greenhithe

FUNNEL: *Yellow.*   HULL: *Green with white line and red boot-topping.*
AREA OF OPERATION: *River Thames (Lighterage).*

Britannia	...	...	...	1893	76	360 (B)	M rbt fm SR
ex T. B. Heathorne							

GRIMSBY SALVAGE & TOWAGE CO. LTD.
Grimsby

FUNNEL: HULL: *Black with red boot-topping.*
AREA OF OPERATION: *Grimsby.*

Alfred Bannister	...	...	1964	35	340 (I)	M
Brenda Fisher	...	...	1955	52	360 (I)	M
Herbert Crampin	...	...	1966	44	451 (I)	M
Sir Jack Croft Baker	...	...	1964	35	340 (I)	M
Sir John Marsden	...	...	1964	35	340 (I)	M
Thomas Baskcomb	...	...	1963	35	340 (I)	M
William Grant	...	...	1963	35	340 (I)	M

HOLYHEAD TOWING CO. LTD.
Holyhead

FUNNEL: HULL:
AREA OF OPERATION: *Holyhead and Mersey Approaches.*

Afon Cefni	...	...	...	1951	231	1,120 (I)	SR
ex Applegarth–70							

Afon Goch ... ... ex Scheldt VIII–67, Hengst–64	1939	117	—	M
Afon Wen ... ... ex Rosegarth–70	1954	231	1,120 (I)	SR

M. F. HORLOCK
Mistley

FUNNEL: HULL: *Black.*

AREA OF OPERATION: *Harwich Area.*

Brett	1931	49	—	M

C. HORLOCK
Mistley

FUNNEL: HULL:

AREA OF OPERATION: *Harwich Area.*

Rebel ... ... ex Flanchford–68	—	—	—	M

J. HOWARD & CO. (NORTHERN) LTD.
Liverpool

FUNNEL: *Green with large white letter "H".*   HULL: *Black.*

AREA OF OPERATION: *Contract work, presently in the Mersey.*

Amanda Howard ... ... ex Sir Bevois–68	1953	318	1,500 (I)	SR(2)
Kinghow ... ... ex Charles Hearn–67	1959	139	740 (B)	M(2)
Lady Howard	1968	151	—	M

THE HULL STEAM TRAWLERS MUTUAL INSURANCE & PROTECTING CO. LTD.
Hull

FUNNEL: *Yellow with black top.*   HULL: *Black.*

AREA OF OPERATION: *Hull Fish Docks.*

Aurora	1963	50	385 (B)	M/VS
Neptune	1966	50	385 (B)	M/VS
Triton	1964	50	385 (B)	M/VS
Zephyr	1964	50	385 (B)	M/VS

HUMPHREY & GREY (LIGHTERAGE) LTD.
London

FUNNEL: *Black with broad red band bordered by two narrow white bands.* HULL: *Black with white line and red boot-topping.*

AREA OF OPERATION: *River Thames (Lighterage).*

Friston Down	...	...	...	1964	99	650 (B)	M
Owen Smith	...	...	...	1946	66	450 (B)	M
ex Fossa–61							
Sir Aubrey	...	...	...	1962	59	450 (B)	M
Sir John	...	...	...	1935	83	500 (B)	M rbt fm SR
St. Olaf	...	...	...	1956	37	360 (B)	M

HUSBAND'S SHIPYARDS LTD.
Southampton

FUNNEL: *Yellow with black top and houseflag.* HULL: *Black.*

AREA OF OPERATION: *Southampton Water.*

Adherence	...	...	...	1944	54	400 (B)	M rbt fm SR
ex Tid 75–65							
Affluence	...	...	...	1938	91	450 (B)	M
ex C.10							
Assurance	...	...	...	1944	64	500 (B)	M rbt fm SR
ex Tid 71							

IRVINE HARBOUR CO. LTD
Irvine

FUNNEL: *Maroon with black top.* HULL: *Black with red boot-topping.*

AREA OF OPERATION: *Irvine.*

Garnock	...	...	...	1956	78	324 (B)	M/KN

ITCHEN MARINE TOWAGE LTD.
Southampton

FUNNEL: *Blue with black top.* HULL:

AREA OF OPERATION: *Southampton (Lighterage).*

Testgarth	...	...	...	1937	60	390 (B)	M

Husband's Shipyards Ltd. M.T. ADHERENCE   [*D. Lynch*

JAMES CONTRACTING & SHIPPING CO. LTD.
Southampton

FUNNEL: HULL:

AREA OF OPERATIONS: *Southampton Water and on contract work.*

Foremost Trojan	...	...	1968	72	495 (B)	M
Jumsey ...	...	...	1928	30	180 (B)	M
Snip	...	...	—	—	—	M
Tideall ...	...	...	1943	54	336 (B)	M rbt fm SR
ex Tid 43						
Tideway ...	...	...	1945	54	336 (B)	M rbt fm SR
ex Tid 120						

C. J. KING & SONS, LTD.
Bristol

FUNNEL: *White with black top separated by broad band.* HULL: *Black.*

AREA OF OPERATIONS: *Avonmouth and Bristol Channel.*

Sea Alarm	...	...	1941	263	1,000 (I)	SR
ex Flying Fulmar–56, Empire Ash–46						
Sea Alert	...	...	1960	168	600 (B)	M
Sea Challenge	...	...	1967	185	1,100 (B)	M
Sea Merrimac	...	...	1964	163	920 (B)	M
Sea Queen	...	...	1944	244	1,000 (I)	SR
ex Empire Walter–47						
Sea Volunteer	...	...	1963	163	920 (B)	M

KINGS LYNN CONSERVANCY BOARD
Kings Lynn

FUNNEL: *Yellow with black top.*   HULL: *Grey with white line and red boot-topping.*
AREA OF OPERATIONS: *Kings Lynn.*

Conservator K. L.	...	...	1963	42	—	M

J. P. KNIGHT LTD.
Rochester

FUNNEL: *Black with two white bands above white letter "K".*   HULL: *Black with white line and red boot-topping.*
AREA OF OPERATIONS: *Rivers Thames and Medway and Coastal Towage.*

J. P. Knight Ltd., Rochester							
Kelvedon ...	...	...	...	1940	41	300 (B)	M
ex Keston–69							
Kemsing	...	...	...	1960	135	1,000 (B)	M
Kenley	...	...	...	1958	246	1,500 (B)	M/F
Kennet	...	...	...	1965	278	1,810 (B)	M/K
Keston	...	...	...	1970	299	3,000 (B)	M/K/F
Kestrel	...	...	...	1955	223	1,150 (B)	M/F
Keverne	...	...	...	1960	260	1,650 (B)	M/K/F
Kent	...	...	...	1948	121	880 (B)	M
Kite	...	...	...	1952	118	960 (B)	M
Knighton ...	...	...	...	1968	280	1,810 (B)	M/K
J. P. Knight Ltd., London:							
Kara	...	...	...	1935	56	390 (B)	M
ex Landay							
Katra	...	...	...	1936	68	520 (B)	M
Kawara	...	...	...	1934	74	455 (B)	M
Khurda	...	...	...	1930	50	495 (B)	M
Kitava	...	...	...	1953	77	550 (B)	M
ex Silvergilt–71, Esso Greenwich—66							
Kokoda	...	...	...	1954	77	550 (B)	M
ex Silverclad–71, Esso Reading–66							
Kundah	...	...	...	1936	69	520 (B)	M

J. H. LAMEY, LTD.
Liverpool
SEE ALEXANDRA TOWING CO. LTD.

LIVERPOOL SCREW TOWING & LIGHTERAGE CO. LTD.
Liverpool
SEE ALEXANDRA TOWING CO LTD.

J. P. Knight Ltd.   M.T. KNIGHTON   *[M. J. Gaston*

Liverpool Grain Storage & Transit Co.   M.T. CERES   *[P. C. White*

LIVERPOOL GRAIN STORAGE & TRANSIT CO. LTD.
Liverpool

FUNNEL: *Blue with black badge.* HULL: *Black.*
AREA OF OPERATIONS: *Liverpool (Lighterage).*

Castor	1944	54	—	M
ex Tidworth–66, Tid 116				
Ceres	1961	43	—	M

LONDON & ROCHESTER TRADING CO. LTD.
Rochester

FUNNEL: *Black with silver crescent on broad red band between two narrow white bands.* HULL: *Light brown with two white lines and red boot-topping.*
AREA OF OPERATION: *River Medway (Lighterage).*

Dragette	1947	50	300 (B)	M

LONDON TUGS LTD.
London

FUNNEL: *Black with original Dick & Page houseflag on broad red band.* HULL: *Black with white line and red boot-topping.*
AREA OF OPERATION: *River Thames and Coastal towage.*

Avenger	1962	300	2,250 (B)	M/K
Burma	1966	165	1,360 (B)	M
Cervia	1946	233	900 (I)	SR
ex Empire Raymond–47				
Challenge	1931	212	1,150 (I)	SR
Contest	1933	213	1,150 (I)	SR
Culex	1958	98	660 (B)	M
Dhulia	1959	272	1,600 (B)	M
Fossa	1961	83	1,000 (B)	M
Hibernia	1962	300	2,250 (I)	SR/K
Ionia	1960	120	1,360 (B)	M
Moorcock	1959	273	1,600 (B)	M
Napia	1943	261	1,200 (I)	SR
ex Empire Jester–46				
Rana	1951	99	700 (B)	M
Sun II	1965	145	1,350 (B)	M
Sun III	1966	145	1,350 (B)	M
Sun XVIII	1951	105	640 (I)	M
Sun XIX	1956	192	1,210 (B)	M
Sun XX	1957	192	1,210 (B)	M
Sun XXI	1959	183	1,316 (B)	M
Sun XXII	1960	183	1,316 (B)	M
Sun XXIII	1961	145	1,340 (B)	M
Sun XXIV	1962	120	1,000 (I)	M
Sun XXV	1963	215	2,400 (I)	M/K
Sun XXVI	1964	215	2,400 (I)	M/K
Sun XXVII	1968	225	2,400 (I)	M/K

London & Rochester Trading Co.   M.T. DRAGETTE   [*John G. Callis*

London Tugs Ltd.   S.T. HIBERNIA   [*M. J. Gaston*

London Tugs Ltd.   M.T. SUN XXVII   [*M. J. Gaston*

M. B. DREDGING CO. LTD.
London

FUNNEL: *Grey with white-edged blue pennant houseflag.*   HULL: *Black.*
AREA OF OPERATION: *River Thames or on contract work.*

Pushman ...	...	...	...	1970	38	574 (B)	M/Pusher
Thrush ...	...	...	...	1952	75	400 (B)	M
ex *Teal, Gull*							

M.N.S. (FISHING) LTD.
Newhaven, Sussex

FUNNEL: *Black with "Metrec" symbol.*   HULL: *Black.*
AREA OF OPERATION: *Newhaven and on contract work.*

Dagger ...	...	...	...	—	—	—	—
ex *Hillman, Tid 79*							
Mallard ...	...	...	—	—	—	—	
ex *M.S.C. Mallard*							

MANCHESTER SHIP CANAL COMPANY
Manchester

FUNNEL: *Black with two narrow white bands.* HULL: *Black.*
AREA OF OPERATION: *Manchester Docks and Ship Canal.*

M.S.C. Onset	...	...	...	1947	154	1,200 (B)	M(2)
M.S.C. Onward	...	...	...	1948	154	1,200 (B)	M(2)
M.S.C. Panther	...	...	...	1950	154	1,200 (B)	M(2)
M.S.C. Puma	...	...	...	1950	154	1,200 (B)	M(2)
M.S.C. Quarry	...	...	...	1951	154	1,200 (B)	M(2)
M.S.C. Quest	...	...	...	1951	154	1,200 (B)	M(2)
M.S.C. Ranger	...	...	...	1952	154	1,200 (B)	M(2)
M.S.C. Rover	...	...	...	1952	154	1,200 (B)	M(2)
M.S.C. Sabre	...	...	...	1956	147	1,440 (B)	M(2)
M.S.C. Sceptre	...	...	...	1956	147	1,290 (B)	M(2)
M.S.C. Scimitar	...	...	...	1956	147	1,290 (B)	M(2)
M.S.C. Sovereign	...	...	...	1957	147	1,290 (B)	M(2)
M.S.C. Talisman	...	...	...	1961	124	1,210 (B)	M(2)
M.S.C. Tarn	...	...	...	1961	124	1,210 (B)	M(2)
M.S.C. Ulex	...	...	...	1965	127	1,300 (B)	M(2)
M.S.C. Undine	...	...	...	1966	127	1,300 (B)	M(2)
Dredging Tugs:							
M.S.C. Daphne	...	...	...	1954	83	140 (B)	M
M.S.C. Diana	...	...	...	1956	84	140 (B)	M
M.S.C. Deborah	...	...	...	1958	35	140 (B)	M
M.S.C. Dido	...	...	...	1959	35	140 (B)	M
M.S.C. Dainty	...	...	...	1959	37	140 (B)	M
M.S.C. Daring	...	...	...	1959	37	140 (B)	M
M.S.C. Dawn	...	...	...	1960	37	140 (B)	M

W. G. MARRIOTT
London

FUNNEL: *Cream with narrow black top.* HULL: *Black.*
AREA OF OPERATION: *River Thames (Lighterage).*

William George	...	...	1949	—	—	M

MERCANTILE LIGHTERAGE LTD.
London
SEE WM. CORY GROUP

MINISTRY OF DEFENCE (NAVY)
London

FUNNEL: *Royal Marine Auxiliary Service: Grey, or grey with black top, with or without tethered Seahorse motif. Port Auxiliary Service: Yellow with black top separated by white over blue over white bands.* HULL: *R.M.A.S. Black. P.A.S. Black with white topline and red boot-topping.*

AREAS OF OPERATION: *Chatham, Plymouth and Devonport, Portsmouth, Portland, Rosyth, Clyde, and at overseas bases.*

Royal Marine Auxiliary Service:

Agile	...	...	...	...	1958	641	1,600 (B)	M(2)
Bustler	...	...	...	...	1942	1,100	3,020 (B)	M
Cyclone	...	...	...	...	1943	1,100	3,020 (B)	M

ex *Welshman–65, Castle Peak–62, Caroline Moller–54, Growler–52*

Eminent	...	...	...	...	1946	295	800 (I)	SR

ex *Empire*

Reward	...	...	...	...	1945	1,136	3,020 (B)	M
Robust	...	...	...	...	1971	900	4,500 (B)	M(2)
Roysterer	...	...	...	...	1970	900	4,500 (B)	M(2)
Rollicker	...	...	...	...	1971	900	4,500 (B)	M(2)
Samsonia	...	...	...	...	1942	1,100	3,020 (B)	M

ex *Foundation Josephine–52, Samsonia–48, Samson*

Typhoon	...	...	...	...	1959	1,034	2,880 (B)	M

Port Auxiliary Service:

Accord	...	...	...	...	1957	760	1,600 (B)	M(2)
Advice	...	...	...	...	1957	760	1,600 (B)	M(2)
Agatha	...	...	...	...	1961	38	400 (B)	M
Agnes	...	...	...	...	1961	38	400 (B)	M
Airedale	...	...	...	...	1961	152	1,320 (B)	M(2)
Alice	...	...	...	...	1961	38	400 (B)	M
Alsation	...	...	...	...	1961	152	1,320 (B)	M(2)
Audrey	...	...	...	...	1961	38	400 (B)	M
Barbara	...	...	...	...	1963	38	400 (B)	M
Basset	...	...	...	...	1963	152	1,320 (B)	M(2)

ex *Beagle–68*

Betty	...	...	...	...	1963	38	400 (B)	M
Boxer	...	...	...	...	1963	152	1,320 (B)	M(2)
Brenda	...	...	...	...	1963	38	400 (B)	M
Bridget	...	...	...	...	1963	38	400 (B)	M
CD 5	...	...	...	...	1945	56	350 (B)	M
Cairn	...	...	...	...	1964	152	1,320 (B)	M(2)
Capable	...	...	...	...	1946	832	3,000 (I)	SR(2)
Careful	...	...	...	...	1945	832	3,000 (I)	SR(2)
Chainshot	...	...	...	...	1945	56	350 (B)	M
Charlotte	...	...	...	...	1968	69	650 (B)	M
Christine	...	...	...	...	1968	69	650 (B)	M
Clare	...	...	...	...	1968	79	600 (B)	M
Collie	...	...	...	...	1964	152	1,320 (B)	M(2)
Confiance	...	...	...	...	1955	760	1,600 (B)	M(2)
Confident	...	...	...	...	1956	760	1,600 (B)	M(2)
Corgi	...	...	...	...	1964	152	1,320 (B)	M(2)
Daisy	...	...	...	...	1968	69	650 (B)	M
Dalmatian	...	...	...	...	1965	153	1,320 (B)	M(2)
Daphne	...	...	...	...	1968	69	650 (B)	M
Deerhound	...	...	...	...	1965	152	1,320 (B)	M(2)
Dexterous	...	...	...	...	1957	473	1,600 (B)	ME(PW)
Director	...	...	...	...	1957	473	1,600 (B)	ME(PW)
Doris	...	...	...	...	1969	69	650 (B)	M
Dorothy	...	...	...	...	1968	79	600 (B)	M
Edith	...	...	...	...	1969	79	600 (B)	M
Elkhound	...	...	...	...	1965	152	1,320 (B)	M(2)
Empire Fred	...	...	...	...	1942	234	900 (I)	SR
Empire Rosa	...	...	...	...	1946	292	900 (I)	SR
Faithful	...	...	...	...	1957	473	1,600 (B)	ME(PW)

Felicity	...	...	...	...	1968	72	600 (B)	M/VS
Forceful	...	...	...	...	1957	473	1,600 (B)	ME(PW)
Grapeshot	...	...	...	...	1945	57	370 (B)	M
Grinder	...	...	...	...	1958	473	1,600 (B)	ME(PW)
Griper	...	...	...	...	1958	473	1,600 (B)	ME(PW)
Husky	...	...	...	...	1969	152	1,320 (B)	M(2)
Labrador	...	...	...	...	1966	152	1,320 (B)	M(2)
Mastiff	...	...	...	...	1968	152	1,320 (B)	M(2)
Pointer	...	...	...	...	1966	152	1,320 (B)	M(2)
Prompt	...	...	...	...	1943	232	900 (I)	SR
ex Warden–51, Empire Spitfire–47								
Resolve	...	...	...	...	1946	290	800 (I)	SR
ex Empire Zona–59								
Saluki	...	...	...	...	1968	152	1,320 (B)	M(2)
Samson	...	...	...	...	1954	855	3,000 (I)	SR(2)
Sea Giant	...	...	...	...	1955	855	3,000 (I)	SR(2)
Sealyham	...	...	...	...	1968	152	1,320 (B)	M(2)
Setter	...	...	...	...	1969	152	1,320 (B)	M(2)
Sheepdog	...	...	...	...	1968	152	1,320 (B)	M(2)
Spaniel	...	...	...	...	1968	152	1,320 (B)	M(2)
Superman	...	...	...	...	1954	855	3,000 (I)	SR(2)
Tanac 35	...	...	...	...	1944	55	270 (B)	M
Tanac 83	...	...	...	...	1944	55	270 (B)	M
Tanac 121	...	...	...	...	1944	55	270 (B)	M
Tid 3	...	...	...	...	1944	55	220 (I)	SR
Tid 99	...	...	...	...	1943	55	220 (I)	SR
Tid 145	...	...	...	...	1943	55	220 (I)	SR
Tid 164	...	...	...	...	1943	55	220 (I)	SR
Tid 172 (W.92)	...	...	...	1943	55	220 (I)	SR

Ministry of Defence M.T. FELICITY

[*John G. Callis*

Ministry of Defence   M.T. CHAINSHOT   [*M. J. Gaston*

Ministry of Defence   M.T. MASTIFF   *M. J. Gaston*

NEW MEDWAY STEAM PACKET CO. LTD.
Rochester

FUNNEL: HULL:

AREA OF OPERATION: *River Medway.*

Acorn	1934	32	105 (B)	M
ex Hooligan–70				

R. G. ODELL LTD.
London

FUNNEL: *Black with blue letter "O" on white band.*   HULL: *Black with two white lines and red boot-topping.*

AREA OF OPERATION: *River Thames (Lighterage).*

Churchill	1910	70	480 (B)	M rbt fm SR
ex Denton–53, Mary Blake				
Union	1895	48	—	M rbt fm SR

F. OLDHAM
Liverpool

FUNNEL: HULL:

AREA OF OPERATION:

Martin Oldfield	1942	—	—	—
ex Edith Lamey–69, Robert Hamilton, C.618				

OVERSEAS TOWAGE & SALVAGE CO. LTD.
(ASSOCIATED WITH L. SMIT & CO'S INTERNATIONALE SLEEPDIENST)
London

FUNNEL: *Black with broad blue band.*   HULL: *Black with white line and red boot-topping.*

AREA OF OPERATION: *Ocean Towage and salvage.*

Sheilia	1940	52	450 (I)	M
ex Wachtel				

J. T. PALMER & SONS
London

FUNNEL: *Blue with black top and white letter "P".*   HULL: *Dark green with red boot-topping.*

AREA OF OPERATION: *River Thames (Lighterage).*

Niparound	1957	43	202 (B)	M
ex Beckton II–65				

B. PERRY & SONS
Bristol

FUNNEL: *Yellow with black top.*   HULL: *Black with red boot-topping.*
AREA OF OPERATION: *Bristol and Avonmouth (Lighterage).*

Salisbury ... ex B.P.2., Tid 15	...	...	...	1943	45	220 (I)	SR

J. H. PIGOTT & SON, LTD.
Grimsby and Immingham

FUNNEL: *Black with two silver bands.*   HULL: *Black over grey with green boot-topping and yellow line.*
AREA OF OPERATION: *Grimsby, Immingham and Coastal Towage.*

Lady Alma	...	...	...	1966	220	850 (B)	M
Lady Cecilia	...	...	...	1966	198	850 (B)	M
Lady Elsie	...	...	...	1970	263	2,800 (B)	M/K
Lady Laura	...	...	...	1967	114	1,240 (B)	M
Lady Marina	...	...	...	1967	155	1,240 (B)	M
Lady Sarah	...	...	...	1970	263	2,800 (B)	M/K
Lady Sybil...	...	...	...	1964	130	797 (B)	M
Lady Thelma	...	...	...	1966	211	2,024 (B)	M/F
Lady Theresa	...	...	...	1962	150	920 (B)	M
Lady Vera...	...	...	...	1971	225	—	M/K

PORT OF LONDON AUTHORITY
London

FUNNEL: *Yellow, or yellow with black top.*   HULL: *Black with red boot-topping.*
AREAS OF OPERATION: *Ship towage in London and Tilbury Dlocks; Dredging, etc., towage in River Thames.*

River Tugs:							
Broodbank	...	...	...	1966	260	1,000 (B)	M(2)/Pshr
Lord Devonport		...	...	1959	130	935 (B)	M
Lord Ritchie	...	...	...	1960	130	935 (B)	M
Lord Waverley	...	...	...	1960	130	925 (B)	M
Dock Tugs:							
Placard	...	...	...	1966	122	1,600 (B)	M/V
Placer	...	...	...	1967	38	400 (B)	M
Plagal	...	...	...	1951	159	1,200 (B)	M
Plangent	...	...	...	1951	159	1,200 (B)	M/K
Plankton	...	...	...	1966	122	1,600 (B)	M/V
Planter	...	...	...	1967	38	400 (B)	M
Plasible	...	...	...	1968	38	400 (B)	M
Plasma	...	...	...	1965	122	1,600 (B)	M/V
Plateau	...	...	...	1952	159	1,200 (B)	M
Platina	...	...	...	1952	159	1,200 (B)	M
Platonic	...	...	...	1968	38	400 (B)	M
Platoon	...	...	...	1965	122	1,600 (B)	M/V

J. H. Pigott & Son Ltd.   M.T. LADY CECILIA   [*M. J. Gaston*

PORT OF PRESTON AUTHORITY
Preston

FUNNEL: *Black with shield of Preston coat-of-arms in blue and white.* HULL: *Black.*

AREA OF OPERATION: *Preston and River Ribble.*

Frank Jamieson ...	...	...	1956	146	720 (B)	M
Hewitt ...	...	...	1951	137	800 (B)	M
John Herbert	...	...	1955	146	729 (B)	M

POUNDS SHIPOWNERS & SHIPBREAKERS LTD.
Portsmouth

FUNNEL: HULL:

AREA OF OPERATIONS: *Portsmouth.*

Plaboy	...	...	...	...	1957	36	360 (B)	M

REA LTD., and REA TOWING LTD.
Liverpool

FUNNEL: *Red with black top separated by narrow white band and with a white letter "R" in a white-bordered black diamond.* HULL: *Black with white line and red boot-topping.*

AREA OF OPERATION: *Liverpool, Birkenhead and River Mersey.*

Aysgarth	...	...	...	1950	231	1,120 (I)	SR
Beechgarth	...	...	...	1964	207	1,350 (B)	M
Brackengarth	...	...	...	1969	334	—	M/FF
Cedargarth	...	...	...	1962	213	1,300 (B)	M
Cherrygarth	...	...	...	1963	62	—	M
Elmgarth	...	...	...	1960	75	—	M
Foylegarth	...	...	...	1958	208	1,270 (B)	M
ex Foylemore–69							
Grassgarth	...	...	...	1953	231	1,120 (I)	SR
Hazelgarth	...	...	...	1959	230	1,680 (B)	M
Hollygarth	...	...	...	1969	334	—	M/FF
Kilgarth	...	...	...	1958	208	1,270 (B)	M
ex Kilmore–69							
Maplegarth	...	...	...	1961	230	1,350 (B)	M/FF
Pinegarth	...	...	...	1961	63	400 (B)	M
Rossgarth	...	...	...	1958	206	1,270 (B)	M
ex Rossmore–69							
Throstlegarth	...	...	...	1954	231	1,120 (I)	SR
Willowgarth	...	...	...	1959	230	1,680 (B)	M

Rea Ltd.   M.T. BRACKENGARTH   ["*Fotoship*"

W. J. REYNOLDS, LTD.
Torpoint, Cornwall

FUNNEL: *Yellow with black top.* HULL: *Black.*
AREA OF OPERATION: *Plymouth and Devonport.*

Antony	...	...	...	...	1921	137	500 (I)	SR
ex Corgarth–60								
Carbeile	...	...	...	...	1929	110	350 (I)	SR
ex George Livesey								
Tactful	...	...	...	...	1923	124	400 (I)	SR
ex Tolbenny–65, F. T. Everard–51								
Trevol	...	...	...	...	1921	137	650 (I)	SR
ex Reagarth–60								

RIVER WEAR COMMISSIONERS
Sunderland

FUNNEL: *Yellow with black top and black sextant.* HULL: *Black with white line and red boot-topping.*

AREA OF OPERATIONS: *Sunderland and River Wear.*

Biddick	...	...	...	...	1944	54	220 (I)	SR
ex Tid 54								
Pallion	...	...	...	...	1944	54	220 (I)	SR
ex Tid 72								

HARRY ROSE (TOWAGE) LTD.
Poole

FUNNEL: *Red with black top and white letters "H R" in white ring.* HULL: *Black with white line and red boot-topping.*

AREA OF OPERATIONS: *Poole Harbour.*

Wendy Ann	...	...	...	1950	29	350 (I)	M
Wendy Ann 2	...	...	...	1940	44	500 (I)	M

SEAHAM HARBOUR DOCK CO. LTD.
Seaham

FUNNEL: *Black with broad red band.* HULL: *Black with red boot-topping.*
AREA OF OPERATION: *Seaham Harbour.*

Chipchase	...	...	...	1953	126	400 (I)	SR(2)
Conservator	...	...	...	1925	96	387 (I)	SR

SHIPBREAKING (QUEENBOROUGH) LTD.
Sheerness

FUNNEL: HULL:

AREA OF OPERATION: *Sheerness and Queenborough.*

S.Q.L. I	...	1942	131	770 (B)	M(2)
ex M.S.C. Nymph–70					
S.Q.L. 2	...	1941	131	770 (B)	M(2)
ex M.S.C. Neptune–70					

SHOREHAM HARBOUR TRUSTEES
Shoreham, Sussex

FUNNEL: (*None*). HULL: *Black with brown upperworks.*

AREA OF OPERATIONS: *Shoreham.*

Kingston Buci	...	...	...	1960	70	—	M

SMIT & CORY INTERNATIONAL PORT TOWAGE LTD.
London

FUNNEL: *Black with broad white band bearing a yellow shackle device superimposed on a black diamond.* HULL: *Black with red boot-topping.*

AREA OF OPERATION:

Point Melford	...	...	...	1971	300	—	M
Point Tupper	...	...	...	1971	300	—	M

SOUTHAMPTON, ISLE OF WIGHT & SOUTH OF ENGLAND ROYAL MAIL STEAM PACKET CO. LTD.
(RED FUNNEL TUGS)
Southampton

FUNNEL: *Dark red with black top.* HULL: *Black with yellow line and red boot-topping.*

AREA OF OPERATION: *Southampton and the Solent.*

Bonchurch	...	...	...	1944	55	220 (B)	M rbt fm SR
ex Baie Comeau–66, Abeille No 13, Tid 174						
Calshot	...	...	...	1964	475	1,800 (M)	M(2) Tdr
Chale	...	...	...	1965	250	1,300 (B)	M(2)
Culver	...	...	...	1956	246	1,340 (B)	M(2)/K/F
Dunnose	...	...	...	1958	241	1,340 (B)	M(2)
Gatcombe	...	...	...	1970	260	—	M/K/F
Thorness	...	...	...	1953	318	1,340 (B)	M(2)
Vecta	...	...	...	1970	269	—	M/F

See also Coastal Section.

SPILLER'S LTD.
Hull

FUNNEL: HULL:

AREA OF OPERATION: *Hull and River Humber (Lighterage).*

Spiller's Rose	...	...	...	1954	39	—	M

RICHARD TEAL
Newark

FUNNEL: HULL:

AREA OF OPERATION: *Rivers Humber and Trent (Lighterage).*

Allan a Dale	...	...	...	1917	62	—	SR
Forest King	...	...	...	1917	62	—	SR

TEES MARINE SERVICES LTD.
Middlesbrough

FUNNEL: HULL:

AREA OF OPERATION: *Middlesbrough and River Tees.*

Plastron	...	...	...	1953	80	400 (B)	M

TEES AND HARTLEPOOL PORT AUTHORITY
Middlesbrough

FUNNEL: HULL:

AREA OF OPERATIONS: *Middlesbrough and Hartlepools.*

Francis Samuelson	...	...	1924	140	400 (I)	SR
Hart	...	...	...	...	1958	145	1,200 (B)	M
Joanetta	...	...	...	...	1911	49	106 (I)	SR
Seaton	...	...	...	...	1959	145	1,200 (B)	M
Stranton	...	...	...	...	1958	145	1,200 (B)	M
Wilton	...	...	...	...	1955	208	—	M

TEES TOWING CO. LTD.
Middlesbrough

FUNNEL: *Red with black top and two widely-spaced white bands.* HULL: *Black with yellow line and red boot-topping.*

AREA OF OPERATIONS: *Middlesbrough and Coastal/Short Sea Towage.*

Ayton Cross	...	...	...	1967	214	2,000 (B)	M/K
Banbury Cross	...	...	...	1958	106	750 (B)	M
Danby Cross	...	...	...	1961	120	750 (B)	M/K
Erimus Cross	...	...	...	1960	192	1,200 (B)	M
Fiery Cross	...	...	...	1957	192	1,200 (B)	M/KF
Leven Cross	...	...	...	1971	160	1,250 (B)	M/KF
Marton Cross	...	...	...	1963	150	1,100 (B)	M
Ormesby Cross	...	...	...	1967	230	1,800 (B)	M/K

THAMES & GENERAL LIGHTERAGE CO. LTD.
London

FUNNEL: *Blue with red top and large white letter "T".* HULL: *Black with white line and red boot-topping.*

AREA OF OPERATIONS: *River Thames (Lighterage).*

General VI	...	...	...	1946	50	390 (B)	M
ex Mick, Caledonian							
General VII	...	...	...	1962	63	665 (B)	M
General VIII	...	...	...	1965	77	1,000 (B)	M
Robertsbridge	...	...	...	1937	90	450 (B)	M
Wortha	...	...	...	1929	96	405 (B)	M

TYNE TUGS LTD.
Newcastle

FUNNEL: *Red with black top.* HULL: *Black with red boot-topping.*

AREA OF OPERATIONS: *River Tyne and Coastal Towage.*

Tyne Tugs Ltd. is the operating company of tugs owned by three separate concerns as listed below.

France, Fenwick Tyne & Wear Co. Ltd.							
Alnmouth	...	...	...	1962	170	950 (B)	M
Alnwick	...	...	...	1955	119	1,086 (B)	M
Ashbrooke	...	...	...	1955	119	1,086 (B)	M
Bamburgh	...	...	...	1954	119	1,086 (B)	M
George V	...	...	...	1915	224	1,086 (B)	M rbt fm SR
Lawson-Batey Tugs Ltd.							
Appelsider	...	...	...	1962	175	1,000 (B)	M
Ironsider	...	...	...	1967	156	1,320 (B)	M
Northsider	...	...	...	1967	170	1,000 (B)	M
Quaysider	...	...	...	1955	157	1,200 (B)	M
Roughsider	...	...	...	1958	143	750 (B)	M
Westsider	...	...	...	1964	151	986 (B)	M
Ridley Tugs Ltd.:							
Impetus	...	...	...	1954	141	750 (B)	M

UNITED TOWING LTD.
Hull

FUNNEL: *White with black top.* HULL: *Black with white line and green boot-topping.*

AREAS OF OPERATION: *Hull Area; Coastal, Short-Sea and Ocean Towage.*

Bargeman	...	...	...	1955	37	400 (I)	M
ex Brentonian							
Dockman	...	...	...	1949	68	650 (I)	M
ex Stamford Brook							
Englishman	...	...	...	1965	574	4,100 (I)	M(2)
Euroman	...	...	...	1967	1,139	7,500 (I)	M
ex Bremen—72							
Foreman ~~SEA BRISTOLIAN (BA)~~				1959	227	1,200 (I)	M
Headman	...	...	...	1963	193	1,650 (I)	M(2)
Irishman	...	...	...	1966	450	5,000 (I)	M(2)
Keelman	...	...	...	1958	37	400 (I)	M
ex Scorcher							
Krooman	...	...	...	1938	230	1,100 (I)	M
Lighterman	...	...	...	1954	37	400 (I)	M
ex Jaycee							
Lloydsman	...	...	...	1971	2,000	16,000 (B)	M
Masterman	...	...	...	1964	229	1,800 (I)	M(2)
Motorman	...	...	...	1965	98	1,000 (I)	M
Norman	...	...	...	1929	222	1,100 (I)	M
Patrolman	...	...	...	1953	68	680 (I)	M
ex Colne Brook							
Pressman	...	...	...	1950	68	680 (I)	M
ex Tyburn Brook							
Prizeman	...	...	...	1925	226	1,100 (I)	M
Riverman	...	...	...	1963	93	1,100 (I)	M
Scotsman	...	...	...	1929	222	1,100 (I)	M
Seaman	...	...	...	1966	265	2,500 (I)	M(2)
Statesman*	...	...	...	1966	1,167	*10,000 (I)*	M(2)
ex Alice L. Moran—69							
Superman	...	...	...	1967	265	2,500 (I)	M(2)
Tidesman	...	...	...	1963	98	1,000 (I)	M(2)
Tradesman	...	...	...	1964	230	2,500 (I)	M(2)
Trawlerman	...	...	...	1963	98	1,000 (I)	M(2)
Tugman	...	...	...	1964	98	1,000 (I)	M(2)
Waterman	...	...	...	1966	50	400 (I)	M
Welshman	...	...	...	1966	450	5,000 (I)	M(2)
Workman	...	...	...	1963	193	1,650 (I)	M(2)
Yorkshireman	...	...	...	1967	251	—	M(2)

*Chartered from Moran Towing Corp., New York. (Liberian flag). *SOLD TO UNITED 1972*

VOKINS & CO. LTD.
London

FUNNEL: *Dark blue with red letter "V" on large white disc.* HULL: *Black with white line and red boot-topping.*

AREA OF OPERATION: *River Thames (Lighterage).*

Vanoc	...	...	...	1937	58	390 (B)	M
Vista	...	...	...	1940	71	420 (B)	M
Voracious	...	...	...	1929	64	500 (B)	M rbt fm SR
ex Gull							
Vortex	...	...	...	1947	77	465 (B)	M
ex Snowcem							

WELLAND RIVER CATCHMENT BOARD
Peterborough

FUNNEL: *Yellow with black top.* HULL: *Black.*
AREA OF OPERATION: *River Welland Area.*

W. D. B. Tug No 2	...	...	1931	36	—	M

WESTMINSTER DREDGING CO. LTD.
London

FUNNEL: *Black with houseflag.* HULL: *Black.*
AREA OF OPERATION: *River Thames (Dredging towage). Other self-propelled dredging craft work in the Thames, Mersey and on various world-wide contracts.*

Beaver Crest	...	...	...	1966	—	—	M
Pullwell	...	...	...	1954	49	—	M

JOHN H. WHITAKER (HOLDINGS) LTD.
Hull

FUNNEL: *Black with separate red over green bands.* HULL: *Black.*
AREA OF OPERATION: *Hull and River Humber.*

Wilberforce	...	...	...	1920	45	—	M

United Towing Co. Ltd. M.T. RIVERMAN [D. Lynch

JAMES A. WHITE & CO. LTD.
Dunfermline

FUNNEL: *Black with maroon band.*   HULL: *Black with red boot-topping.*
AREA OF OPERATION: *Firth of Forth and on salvage contracts.*

Nellie Laud	1913	123	120 (I)	SR/Salv
ex Concrete				
Recovery	1899	194	384 (I)	SR/Salv
ex Chivelstone				

W. E. WHITE & SONS, LTD.
London

FUNNEL: *Black with white letter "W".*   HULL: *Black with white line.*
AREA OF OPERATION: *Rivers Thames and Medway (Lighterage).*

Boys White ...	1934	—	350 (B)	M
ex Rodney II–68				
Chalky White ...	1934	98	425 (B)	M
ex Abbotsbury				
Doris White	1930	40	500 (B)	M
ex Prima				
Irande ...	1929	96	340 (B)	M
John White ...	1937	88	500 (B)	M
ex Silvermark–66				
Jolly White	1926	34	135 (B)	M
ex Jolly Tar–67				
Keith White	1940	83	520 (B)	M
ex Silvertown–65				

W. E. White & Sons Ltd.   S.T. JOHN WHITE   *M. J. Gaston*

W. E. WHITE & SONS LTD. *continued*

Knocker White ... ... *ex Cairnrock*			1924	96	—	M
Lash White ... ... *ex Lady Vera–69, Brahman–62*			1938	230	850 (I)	SR
Lily White ... ... *ex Balna*			1929	38	300 (B)	M
Louisa White			1949	39	300 (B)	M
Pusher White* ... ... *ex Framfield–69*			1935	—	—	M
Sarah White ... ... *ex Henri*			1925	34	280 (B)	M
William White ... ... *ex Frank–53*			1915	30	120 (B)	M rbt fm SR

*In process of rebuilding as pusher tug.

D. WILLIAMS & CO. LTD.
Swansea

FUNNEL: HULL:

AREA OF OPERATION: *Swansea and on contract work.*

Red Branch ... ... *ex Bessey*			1927	60	—	M

WILLIAMS SHIPPING CO. LTD.
Southampton

FUNNEL: HULL:

AREA OF OPERATION: *Southampton and the Solent (Lighterage).*

Willanne			1932	38	—	M

WIMPEY (MARINE) LTD.
London

FUNNEL: HULL:

AREA OF OPERATION: *Contract work in various districts.*

Andy Mitchell			1968	243	—	M(2)
G.W. 94 ... ... *ex Ireland–65*			1944	84	—	M
G.W. 122 ... ... *ex Neptunus–67*			1947	108	—	M
G.W. 180 ... ... *ex Tregarth–70, Neylandia–61*			1958	102	500 (B)	M

WORKINGTON DOCK & HARBOUR BOARD
Workington

FUNNEL: *Black with broad white band.* HULL: *Black.*

AREA OF OPERATION: *Workington, Cumberland.*

Solway ... ... *ex Empire Ann–48*			1943	232	900 (I)	SR

Irish Republic

CORK HARBOUR COMMISSIONERS
Cork

FUNNEL: *White with black top.* HULL: *Black with white line and red boot-topping.*
AREA OF OPERATION: *Cork and River.*

Richard Wallace	1944	54	220 (I)	SR
ex Zed, Tid 108				
Shandon	1959	109	1,000 (B)	M
ex Flying Dolphin–68				

DUBLIN PORT & DOCKS BOARD
Dublin

FUNNEL: *Yellow with black top.* HULL: *Black with white lines and red boot-topping.*

AREA OF OPERATION: *Dublin and River Liffey.*

Ben Eader	1932	228	1.000 (I)	SR
ex Foremost 84–33				
Cluain Tarbh	1963	286	1,268 (B)	M
Coliemore	1926	244	850 (I)	SR
ex Foremost 42–33				

HENRY & CO. LTD.
Waterford

FUNNEL: HULL:
AREA OF OPERATION: *Waterford and River Suir.*

Gnat	1934	66	390 (B)	M

NORTHERN SLIPWAY LTD.
Dublin

FUNNEL: HULL:
AREA OF OPERATION:

Brambles	1942	242	1,100 (I)	SR
ex Empire Teak–50				
Meadow	1942	238	1,000 (I)	SR
ex Empire Meadow–47				
Piper	1942	250	1,000 (I)	SR
ex Empire Piper–47				

TRAWLERS

ABUNDA FISHING CO. LTD.
Grimsby
FUNNEL: *Blue with gold trident, black top.*   HULL: *Black with red boot-topping.*

Name	Port Registry	Date	Gross Tons	Engines
Belgium	GY.218	1956	577	M

DEPT. OF AGRICULTURE & FISHERIES FOR SCOTLAND
Edinburgh
FUNNEL: HULL:

Fishery Research Vessel: **Scotia**	1971	—	—	M

ALBERT FISHING CO. LTD.
Hartlepools
FUNNEL: *Red with black top and red pennant houseflag.*   HULL:

Moreleigh ... ... ex Iago–59	HL.160	1946	117	M

ALFRED BANNISTER (TRAWLERS) LTD.
Grimsby
FUNNEL: *Houseflag on black.*   HULL: *Black with red boot-topping.*

Saxon Forward	GY.688	1962	204	M
Saxon Onward	GY.618	1960	210	M
Forward Steam Fishing Co. Ltd.:				
Saxon Progress	GY.655	1961	197	M
Saxon Venture	GY.616	1960	211	M
Saxon Trawlers Ltd.:				
Saxon Ranger* .. .. ex Atlantic Seal–65	GY.1396	1961	290	DE

*Stern Trawler

BLAIR & DONNAN
Portavogie
FUNNEL: HULL:

Ranworth Queen	LT.176	1955	181	M

144

BOSTON DEEP SEAS FISHERIES LTD.

(BASIL A. PARKES)

Fleetwood, Grimsby and Lowestoft

FUNNEL: *Red, with or without black top.* HULL: *Black with white line and red boot-topping.*

Boston Beverley	...	...		1971	700	M
Boston Blenheim*	...	...	1971	—	700	M
Boston Comanche	...	...	GY.144	1959	616	M
ex Saint Louis–68						
Boston Comet	...	...	LT.183	1960	137	M
Boston Concord	...	...	GY.730	1965	758	M
Boston Explorer...	...	...	FD.15	1965	425	M
ex Aberdeen Explorer–68						
Boston Harrier	...	...	LT.76	1956	239	M
ex Acadia Snowbird–68, Launched as Boston Britannia						
Boston Lightning	...	...	FD.14	1961	391	M
ex Admiral Burnett–68						
Boston Sea Dart*	...	...	—	1971	150	M
Boston Sea Hawk*	...	...	1971	—	700	M
Boston Trident	...	...	LT.474	1957	182	M
ex John O'Heugh–63						
Boston Valetta	...	...	LT.256	1956	239	M
ex Acadia Fin-Fare–68 Boston, Valetta–61						
Boston Wasp	...	...	GY.639	1960	300	M
Boston York*	...	...	H.3	1968	846	M
D. B. Finn ...	...	...	H.332	1961	701	M
Lady Parkes*	...	...	H.397	1966	1,033	M
Princess Anne	...	...	FD.15	1955	421	M
St. Chad	...	...	H.20	1956	575	M
Sir Fred Parkes*	...	...	H.385	1966	1,033	M
Ssafa	...	...	FD.155	1958	416	M
Aberdeen Near Water Trawlers Ltd.:						
Boston Argosy	...	...	LT.364	1960	195	M
Boston Coronet ...	...	...	LT.459	1959	199	M
Boston Scimitar ...	...	...	LT.100	1959	134	M
Boston Victor	...	...	LT.473	1959	190	M
ex Woodside–63						
Brixham Trawlers, Ltd.:						
Boston Buccaneer	...	...	LT.157	1961	165	M
Boston Seafire	...	...	FD.109	1956	314	M
ex Buzzard–61						
Hawfinch	...	...	FD.114	1956	314	M
Carry On Fishing Co. Ltd.:						
Boston Corsair	...	...	LT.148	1959	134	M
Eton Fishing Co. Ltd.:						
Boston Phantom	...	...	FD.252	1965	431	M
Fleetwood Near Water Trawlers, Ltd.:						
Boston Caravelle	...	...	LT.59	1954	166	M
ex Diadem–63						
Boston Viscount	...	...	LT.509	1965	174	M
Grimsby Near Water Trawlers, Ltd.:						
Boston Javelin	...	...	LT.429	1959	211	M
ex Highland Lady–64						
Boston Shackleton	...	...	LT.714	1960	310	M
ex Haselbeach–67						
Boston Vulcan	...	...	LT.475	1955	182	M
ex St Hilda–63						
Looker Fishing Co. Ltd.:						
Boston Beaver	...	...	LT.445	1962	165	M
Boston Mosquito	...	...	LT.373	1943	118	M
ex Betty Leslie–61						

BOSTON DEEP SEA FISHERIES LTD. continued

Near Water Trawlers, Ltd.:

Boston Widgeon	...	...	LT.427	1961	165	M

Parbel-Smith Ltd.:

Boston Seafoam	...	...	FD.42	1956	398	M
Prince Philip	...	...	FD.400	1963	442	M
William Wilberforce	...	...	H.200	1959	698	M

B. A. Parkes:

Boston Kestrel	...	...	FD.256	1966	431	M

Weelsby Trawlers, Ltd.:

Boston Viking	...	...	LT.510	1965	174	M

Robin Trawlers, Ltd.:

Boston Provost	...	...	LT.274	1960	200	M
Prince Charles	...	...	H.249	1958	691	M

F. & T. Ross, Ltd.:

Boston Whirlwind	...	...	LT.454	1962	165	M

St. Andrew's Steam Fishing Co. Ltd.:

Boston Lincoln*	...	...	GY.1399	1968	846	M
Boston Wayfarer	...	...	LT.508	1965	174	M

*Stern Trawler.
See also Iago Steam Trawler Co. Ltd. Also Fleetwood Tankers, Ltd. in Coastal Section.

BOYD LINE LTD.
Hull

FUNNEL: *White with black top and two red bands.* HULL: *Black with red band and red boot-topping.*

Arctic Avenger	H.118	1956	806	SR
ex Ross Columbia–67, Cape Columbia–66				
Arctic Brigand	H.52	1955	793	SR
ex Marbella–65				
Arctic Buccaneer ...	H.516	1948	613	SR
ex St Bartholomew–52				
Arctic Cavalier	H.204	1960	764	M
Arctic Corsair	H.320	1960	764	M
Arctic Freebooter* ...	H.362	1965	1,633	M
Arctic Galliard	H.209	1952	790	SR
ex Kirkella–63				
Arctic Privateer* ...	H.441	1968	928	M
Arctic Raider*	H.440	1968	928	M
Arctic Ranger	H.155	1957	810	SR
Arctic Vandal	H.344	1961	594	M
Arctic Warrior	H.176	1951	712	SR

*Stern Trawler

BREBNER FISHING CO. LTD.
Aberdeen

FUNNEL: *Yellow with black top.* HULL: *Black with red boot-topping.*

Headway	A.133	1957	174	M

BRUCE'S STORES (ABERDEEN) LTD.
Aberdeen

FUNNEL: *Blue with white letter "B" between two narrow white bands.* HULL: *Dark blue with white line and red boot-topping.*

Cromdale	A.365	1971	119	M
Spinningdale	A.473	1968	103	M

Boston Deep Sea Fisheries Ltd.   M.T. BOSTON JAVELIN

[Port of Lowestoft Research Society

Boston Deep Sea Fisheries Ltd.   M.T. BOSTON SEAFOAM   *[Peter Horsley*

BRITISH UNITED TRAWLERS LTD.
Hull & Grimsby

FUNNEL: HULL:

Black Watch	...	...	...	GY.23	1956	697	RT
Coldstreamer	...	...	...	GY.10	1955	697	RT
Conqueror*	...	...	...	GY.1364	1965	1,157	M
Defiance*	...	...	...	GY.1377	1966	1,113	M
Lord Beatty	...	...	...	H.112	1956	697	RT
Lord Jellicoe	...	...	...	H.228	1962	594	M
Lord Mountevans	...	...	...	H.169	1951	712	SR
Northern Chief ...	...	...	...	GY.128	1950	692	SR
Northern Eagle ...	...	...	...	GY.22	1956	701	SR
Northern Gift	...	...	...	GY.704	1962	590	M
Northern Isles	...	...	...	GY.149	1950	692	SR
Northern Jewel ...	...	...	...	GY.1	1954	799	SR
Northern Prince	...	...	...	GY.121	1950	677	SR
Northern Queen	...	...	...	GY.124	1950	677	SR
Northern Reward	...	...	...	GY.694	1962	655	M
Northern Sceptre	...	...	...	GY.297	1954	804	SR
Northern Sea ...	...	...	...	GY.142	1950	692	SR
Northern Sky ...	...	...	...	GY.427	1956	701	RT
ex Ross Repulse–68, Statham–65							
Northern Sun ...	...	...	...	GY.2	1956	656	SR
ex Wyre Mariner–68							
Royal Lincs	...	...	...	GY.18	1955	697	RT
Vanessa ...	...	...	...	GY.257	1952	661	SR
Velinda ...	...	...	...	GY.29	1956	779	SR
Vianova ...	...	...	...	GY.590	1959	559	SR
Victory* ...	...	...	...	GY.733	1965	1,750	M
Vivaria ...	...	...	...	GY.648	1960	744	M

*Stern Trawler

BRITISH UNITED TRAWLERS (SCOTLAND) LTD.
Granton

FUNNEL: *Blue with letters "B U T" between wavy blue lines on white band.*   HULL: *Blue with white line and red boot-topping.*

Granton Falcon	...	...	GN.16	1956	270	M
Granton Harrier	...	...	GN.77	1962	212	M
Granton Merlin ...	...	...	GN.72	1960	235	M
Granton Osprey...	...	...	GN.19	1960	230	M
Joe Croan	...	...	LH.73	1956	273	M
Malcolm Croan ...	...	...	A.444	1960	234	M
Maureen Croan ...	...	...	A.434	1960	234	M
Netta Croan	...	...	LH.100	1957	268	M
Ardrossan Trawling Co. Ltd.:						
Duff Paton	...	...	GW.3	1956	270	M
Elizabeth Paton ...	...	...	GW.10	1960	220	M
Fairfield ...	...	...	A.361	1962	207	M
Kelso Paton	...	...	GW.2	1956	272	M
Lothian Trawling Co. Ltd.:						
Lothian Leader ...	...	...	GN.18	1959	217	M
Grampian Motor Trawlers Ltd.:						
Schiehallion	...	...	GN.73	1961	243	M

*Stern Trawler

A. J. & A. BUCHAN
Fraserburgh

Ethel Mary	...	...	...	LT.337	1957	134	M

ARTHUR BUCHAN
Peterhead

FUNNEL: HULL:

Loch Kildonan	...	...	...	A.84	1956	149	M

CATCHPOLE & HASHIM
Lowestoft

FUNNEL: *Orange with black top.*   HULL: *Black.*

Dauntless Star	...	...	...	LT.367	1948	133	M
ex Swiftburn–58, Boston Swift–57, Sunlit Waters–52							
Sheriffmuir	...	...	...	LT.313	1952	180	M
Warbler	...	...	...	LT.63	1912	196	M

CEVIC STEAM FISHING CO. LTD.
Fleetwood

FUNNEL: *Black with two red narrow bands.*   HULL: *Black.*

Cevic	...	...	...	FD.241	1958	249	M

COLBY FISH SELLING CO. LTD.
Lowestoft

FUNNEL: *Blue with black top and houseflag.*   HULL: *Black.*

Fellowship	...	...	...	LT.246	1931	127	M

COLNE FISHING CO. LTD.
Lowestoft

FUNNEL: *Blue with black top.*   HULL: *Black or grey.*

Antigua	...	...	...	...	LT.150	1957	204	M
Bahama	...	...	...	...	LT.142	1957	204	M
St Martin	...	...	...	...	LT.376	1961	254	M

Clan Steam Fishing Co. (Grimsby) Ltd.:

Anguilla	...	...	...	...	LT.67	1959	228	M
Barbados	...	...	...	...	LT.312	1958	213	M
Trinidad	...	...	...	...	LT.210	1950	168	M
ex Milford Knight–55								

COLNE FISHING CO. LTD. *continued*

Claridge Trawlers Ltd.:

Bermuda	...	...	...	...	LT.122	1955	205	M
Cuttlefish	...	...	...	...	LT.65	1959	153	M
Kingfish	...	...	...	...	LT.186	1955	151	M
St David's		...	...	...	LT.494	1947	320	M
ex Allan Water–65								
St George's			...	...	LT.403	1946	343	M
ex Thorina–65								
St John	...	...	...	...	LT.7	1969	241	M
St Kitt's	...	...	...	...	LT.481	1941	316	M
ex Postboy–65, Milford Marquis–51								
St Nicola		...	...	...	LT.83	1949	349	M
ex Joli-Fructidor–69, Milford Duchess–54								
St Rose	...	...	...	...	LT.82	1949	349	M
ex Jean Vacquelin–68, Milford Duke–55								
St Thomas	...	...	...	...	LT.8	1969	241	M
Spearfish	...	...	...	...	LT.232	1956	151	M

Dagon Fishing Co. Ltd.:

Grenada	...	...	...	...	LT.130	1955	205	M
Jamaica	...	...	...	...	LT.185	1947	285	M
ex Star of Scotland–60								
St Lucia	...	...	...	...	LT.362	1961	254	M
Sawfish	...	...	...	...	LT.66	1959	153	M

Drifter-Trawlers Ltd.:

Anglerfish	...	...	...	...	LT.391	1961	153	M
Dominica	...	...	...	...	LT.314	1958	213	M

Huxley Fishing Co Ltd.:

Grayfish	...	...	...	...	LT.361	1961	160	M
Montserrat	...	...	...	...	LT.64	1959	228	M
Rockfish	...	...	...	...	LT.244	1956	151	M
Silverfish	...	...	...	...	LT.340	1961	160	M

Colne Fishing Co., Clan Steam Fishing Co., and Dagon Fishing Co. also operate smaller vessels of under 100 g.r.t.

Colne Fishing Co.   M.T. ANTIGUA   [*Port of Lowestoft Research Society*

CONSOLIDATED FISHERIES LTD.
(SIR JOHN R. MARSDEN, BART.)
Grimsby

FUNNEL: *Yellow and red crown on broad white band separating grey from black top.* HULL: *Black with blue line and red boot-topping.*

Arsenal	...	...	...	GY.48	1958	744	SR
Everton	...	...	...	GY.58	1958	884	SR
Grimsby Town	...	...	...	GY.246	1953	711	SR
Hull City	...	...	...	GY.282	1953	711	SR
Rhondda Fishing Co. Ltd.:							
Barnsley	...	...	...	GY.651	1960	441	M
Carlisle	...	...	...	GY.681	1961	441	M
Crystal Palace	...	...	...	GY.683	1961	441	M
Notts Forest	...	...	...	GY.649	1960	441	M
Real Madrid	...	...	...	GY.674	1961	441	M
Wendover Fishing Co. (Grimsby) Ltd.:							
Aldershot	...	...	...	GY.612	1959	427	M
Blackburn Rovers	...	...	...	GY.706	1962	439	M
Gillingham	...	...	...	GY.622	1960	427	M
Huddersfield Town	...	...	...	GY.261	1962	439	M
Port Vale	...	...	...	GY.484	1957	330	M
Spurs	...	...	...	GY.697	1962	450	M

GEORGE CRAIG & SONS, LTD.
Aberdeen

FUNNEL: *Grey with black top separated by narrow red over white bands.* HULL: *Black with white band and red boot-topping.*

Admiral Drake	...	...	A.514	1960	306	M
Admiral Jellicoe	...	...	A.515	1961	306	M
Countesswells	...	...	A.366	1960	190	M
George Craig	...	...	A.203	1957	197	M
Launched as John Watterston						
Grampian Glen	...	...	A.393	1960	211	M
Grampian Hill	...	...	A.517	1961	214	M
River Ness Fishing Co. (1955) Ltd.:						
Admiral Frobisher	...	...	A.159	1957	274	M
Grampian Crest	...	...	A.393	1960	211	M
Mary Craig	...	...	A.263	1959	197	M

CRAIG STORES (ABERDEEN) LTD.
Aberdeen

FUNNEL: *Black with broad blue band between two narrow silver bands.* HULL: *Dark blue with red boot-topping.*

Ardenlea	...	...	A.805	1963	206	M
ex Jarishof–66						
Ashlea	...	...	A.841	1963	308	M
ex Welsh Princess–67						
Birchlea	...	...	A.53	1962	308	M
ex Ross Badger–68, Welsh Consort–67						
Cedarlea	...	...	A.67	1962	308	M
ex Ross Beaver–68, Welsh Monarch–67						

CRAIG STORES (ABERDEEN) LTD. *continued*

Locarno	...	...	...	...	A.850	1959	324	M
ex Longest–65								
Rowanlea	...	...	...	A.832	1963	308	M
ex Welsh Prince–67								
Summerlee	...	...	...	A.577	1956	274	M
Southburn (Seafishing) Ltd.:								
Lindenlea	...	...	...	A.309	1960	281	M

DALBY STEAM FISHING CO. LTD.
Fleetwood

FUNNEL: *Black with white letter "D".* HULL: *Black with red boot-topping.*
HULL: *Black with red boot-topping.*

Jean-Marthe	...	...	...	FD.233	1948	187	M
Vanessa Ann	...	...	...	FD.133	1951	188	M

DEVANHA FISHING CO. LTD.
Aberdeen

FUNNEL: *Red, with white flying bird over large black letter "D". black top.*
HULL: *Black with red boot-topping.*

Carency	...	...	...	...	A.573	1961	209	M
Gilmar	...	...	...	...	A.468	1960	215	M
Kinellen	...	...	...	...	A.578	1961	209	M

DIAMONDS STEAM FISHING CO. LTD.
(H. L. TAYLOR, LTD.)
Grimsby

FUNNEL: *Three white diamonds on broad red band between two narrow blue bands separating yellow from black top.* HULL: *Black with white topline, red boot-topping.*

Erimo	...	...	...	...	GY.691	1962	210	M
Osako	...	...	...	...	GY.600	1958	350	M
Tokio	...	...	...	...	GY.661	1961	331	M
Taylor Fishing Co. Ltd.:								
Hondo	...	...	...	...	GY.668	1961	300	M
Ogano	...	...	...	...	GY.608	1959	350	M
Japan Fishing Co. Ltd.:								
Yesso	...	...	...	GY.610	1958	350	M

C. V. EASTICK, LTD.
Lowestoft

FUNNEL: *Black with houseflag.* HULL: *Black.*

Wilson Line	...	...	...	YH.105	1932	128	M

Dalby Steam Fishing Co.   M.T. JEAN-MARTHE   [*Peter Horsley*

Diamonds Steam Fishing Co.   M.T. YESSO   [*"Fotoship"*

FRESHER FISH, LTD.
Brixham

FUNNEL:			HULL:			
Moonlit Waters	...	...	BM.23	1946	109	M

R. W. GREEVES
Milford Haven

FUNNEL:			HULL:			
Ranworth Queen	...	...	LT.176	1954	181	M

GRIFFITHS & PORTER
Swansea

FUNNEL:				HULL:			
Lord Rodney	...	...	...	A.50	1929	107	M
ex Eugeniusz–49, Lord Rodney–47							

THOMAS HAMLING & CO. LTD.
Hull

FUNNEL: *Yellow with black top separated by broad red band.*   HULL: *Black with red boot-topping.*

St Alcuin	...	...	...	H.125	1950	742	SR
St Britwin	...	...	...	H.124	1950	742	SR
St Dominic	...	...	...	H.116	1958	829	DE
St Gerontius	...	...	...	H.350	1962	659	M
St Giles	...	...	...	H.220	1962	550	M
St Jason*	...	...	...	H.436	1967	1,288	M
St Jasper*	...	...	...	H.31	1968	1,266	M
St Keverne	...	...	...	H.158	1951	794	SR
St Leger	...	...	...	H.178	1951	794	SR
Firth Steam Trawling Co. Ltd.:							
St Amant	...	...	...	H.42	1949	684	SR
ex Swanella–52							
St Apollo	...	...	...	H.592	1948	658	SR

*Stern Trawlers.

ALEXANDER HAY
Aberdeen

FUNNEL: *Yellow with black top separated by silver band.* HULL: *Black.*

Dreadnought	...	...	...	A.377	1960	163	M

HELLYER BROS. LTD.
(BRITISH UNITED TRAWLERS GROUP)
Hull

FUNNEL: *Yellow, with or without black top, with houseflag (White "H" on blue ground).* HULL: *Grey with white line and red boot-topping.*

Benvolio	—	1949	722	SR
Launched as Esmonde				
Brutus	H.29	1949	727	SR
Caesar	H.226	1952	830	SR
Cassio*	H.398	1966	1,574	M
Cariolanus*	H.412	1967	1,105	M
Falstaff	H.107	1959	896	DE
Kingston Almandine ...	H.104	1950	725	SR
ex St. Hubert–51				
Kingston Amber	H.326	1960	785	M
Kingston Beryl	H.128	1959	691	M
Kingston Emerald ...	H.49	1954	811	SR
Kingston Jacinth ...	H.198	1952	794	SR
Kingston Jade	H.149	1951	794	SR
Kingston Onyx	H.140	1950	794	SR
Kingston Pearl	H.127	1958	691	M
Kingston Sapphire ...	H.95	1955	805	SR
Kingston Topaz	H.145	1950	794	SR
Loch Doon	H.101	1949	670	SR
Loch Eriboll	H.323	1960	734	M
Loch Inver	H.110	1950	570	SR
Loch Leven	H.82	1949	670	SR
Loch Moidart	H.481	1947	550	SR
Lord Alexander	H.12	1954	790	SR
Lord Lovat	H.148	1951	713	SR
Lord Nelson*	H.330	1961	1,226	M
Lord St. Vincent ...	H.261	1962	594	M
Lord Tedder	H.154	1951	722	SR
Lorenzo	H.230	1952	830	SR
Macbeth	H.113	1957	810	SR
ex St. Matthew–69, Breughel–61				
Newby Wyke	H.111	1950	672	SR
Orsino†	H.410	1966	1,574	M
Othello	H.581	1937	516	SR
Portia	H.24	1956	883	DE

*Stern Trawler. †Stern Trawler converted to Weather and Mother Ship.

HENRIKSEN & CO. LTD.
Hull

FUNNEL: *Yellow with black top and blue Maltese cross device.* HULL: *Black with red boot-topping.*

Calydon	H.253	1951	787	SR
ex Gullberg–65, Northella–56				
Tarchon	H.152	1957	823	SR
ex Swanella–62				

HEWETT FISHING CO. LTD.
Fleetwood

FUNNEL: *Black with blue houseflag.* HULL: *Grey with blue line and red boot-topping.*

Ella Hewett	...	...	... LO.94	1964	567	M
Kennedy	...	...	... FO.139	1957	426	M
ex Boston Britannia–69						
London Town	...	...	... LO.70	1960	228	M
Robert Hewett	...	...	... LO.65	1930	567	M
Royalist	...	...	... LO.50	1960	228	M

IAGO STEAM TRAWLING CO. LTD.
(BOSTON DEEP SEA FISHERIES GROUP)
Fleetwood

FUNNEL: *Black with narrow black band.* HULL: *Black.*

Broadwater	...	...	... FO.208	1958	426	M
Captain Foley	...	...	... LO.33	1960	434	M
Captain Fremantle	...	...	... LO.22	1959	449	M
Captain Hardy	...	...	... LO.96	1958	444	M
Captain Riou	...	...	... LO.72	1957	391	M
Red Rose	...	...	... LO.36	1956	407	M

RICHARD IRVIN & SONS, LTD.
Aberdeen & N. Shields

FUNNEL: *Black with two red bands.* HULL: *Black.*

Ben Arthur	...	...	... A.742	1960	309	M
ex Lavinda–64						
Ben Bhrackie	...	...	... A.814	1966	443	M
Ben Chourn	...	...	... SN.20	1960	278	M
Ben Gairn	...	...	... A.508	1961	371	M
Ben Glas	...	...	... SN.41	1961	219	M
Ben Gulvain	...	...	... A.751	1965	443	M
Ben Heilem	...	...	... A.553	1961	372	M
Ben Lora	...	...	... SN.43	1961	219	M
Ben Loyal	...	...	... A.256	1958	296	M
Ben Lui	...	...	... —	—	—	—
Ben Meidie	...	...	... A.319	1959	371	M
Ben Screel	...	...	... A.105	1957	293	M
Ben Strome	...	...	... SN.85	1962	280	M
Ben Tarbert	...	...	... A.418	1960	280	M
Ben Torc	...	...	... SN.100	1959	296	M
Ben Vurie	...	...	... SN.33	1961	280	M

H. JAMES
Shetland

FUNNEL: HULL:

Wavecrest	...	...	...	1969	138	M

Hewett Fishing Co.   M.T. ELLA HEWETT

[Peter Horsley

P. & J. JOHNSTONE, LTD.
(SUBSIDIARY OF J. MARR & SONS LTD.)
Aberdeen

FUNNEL: *Red with black top, some with blue letter "J" on white shield.*   HULL: *Black with red boot-topping.*

Gavina	...	...	...	A.871	1953	316	M
Glenstruan	...	...	...	A.200	1958	183	M
Glen Affric	...	...	...	—	1971	117	M
Glen Esk	...	...	...	—	1971	117	M
Navena	...	...	...	FD.172	1959	353	M
Paramount	...	...	...	A.309	1959	250	M
Partisan	...	...	...	A.310	1959	250	M
G. Alexander:							
Bracoden	...	...	...	—	1970	115	M
Forward Motor Trawlers Ltd.:							
Forward Grace	...	...	...	A.531	1961	212	M
Forward Pride	...	...	...	A.367	1960	212	M
Glenstruan Fishing Co. Ltd.:							
Coastal Emperor	...	...	A.456	1960	250	M
Jacamar	...	...	...	A.525	1961	237	M
J. W. Johnstone:							
David John	...	...	...	A.169	1969	110	M
Radiation Fishing Co. Ltd.:							
Radiation	...	...	...	A.115	1957	139	M
J. Watt:							
Steadfast Hope	...	...	...	—	1970	115	M

HUBERT JONES (TRAWLERS) LTD.
Swansea

FUNNEL: *Buff with black top.*   HULL:

Brenda Wilson	...	LT.80	1954	181	M
ex Granby Queen–67					
Georgina Wilson ...	...	HL.10	1955	182	M
ex Fairy Cove–67					
Sally McCabe	...	YH.88	1930	127	M
ex Ocean Vim–55					

W. H. KERR & CO. (SHIPCHANDLERS) LTD.
(BOSTON DEEP SEA FISHERIES LTD. GROUP)
Lowestoft & Milford Haven

FUNNEL: *Red, with or without black top.*   HULL: *Black with white line.*

Deelite	...	YH.29	1929	124		M
ex Ocean Lifebuoy–67						
Deelux	...	YH.84	1930	127		M
ex Ocean Lux–56						
Deeside	...	LT.517	1966	174		M
Dicketa	...	LT.463	1966	174		M
Willing Boys	...	LT.737	1930	147		M

A. W. KING
Aberdeen

FUNNEL: *As below.*   HULL: *Black.*

Hawkstone Fishing Co. Ltd. (Funnel: Cream with silver band and black top):					
Hawkstone	A.530	1961	174		M
Seaward Fishing Co. Ltd. (Funnel: Light blue with houseflag):					
Seaward Petrel	A.412	1959	214		M

H. J. LAMPRELL, LTD.
Lowestoft

FUNNEL: *Various.*   HULL: *Blue or red.*

Fairway	...	LT.206	1958	175	M
Jadestar Glory	...	LT.87	1954	179	M
ex Ludham Queen–70					
Jadestar Gypsy	...	LT.53	1954	179	M
ex Wroxham Queen–70					
Platessa	...	LT.205	1946	112	M

JOHN A. LEWIS
Aberdeen

FUNNEL: *Various*. HULL: *Various*.

Bracondene Fishing Co. Ltd. (Funnel: Red with white band and black top):
Bracondene	...	...	... A.590	1961	215	M

Glendee Fishing Co. Ltd. (Funnel: Yellow with black top):
Eredene	...	...	... A.554	1961	216	M

Malcolm Smith, Ltd. (Funnel: Brown with black top):
Loch Brora	...	...	... A.198	1958	191	M

North Eastern Fisheries, Ltd.:
Mount Eden	...	...	... A.152	1957	294	N

Scottish Motor Trawlers Ltd. (Funnel: Yellow with black top and green thistle device on black disc on white band)
Scottish King	...	...	... A.378	1959	280	M
Scottish Princess	...	...	A.382	1959	280	M
Scottish Queen ...	...	...	A.210	1959	280	M

Seafield Fishing Co. Ltd. (Funnel: Light blue with houseflag).
Mount Everest	...	...	... A.42	1955	303	M

Spey Motor Trawlers Ltd. (Funnel: Grey with silver band and narrow black top).
Speyside	...	...	... A.4	1958	328	M

LINDSEY TRAWLERS LTD. (E. Bacon)
Grimsby

FUNNEL: *Black with white band between two red bands. Hull: Black with red boot-topping.*

Lemberg	...	...	...	GY.664	1961	270	M
Lepanto	...	...	...	GY.662	1961	270	M
Lofoten	...	...	...	GY.684	1962	212	M
Loveden	...	...	...	GY.685	1962	212	M
Lucerne	...	...	...	GY.560	1959	324	M
Tom Grant	...	...	...	GY.1392	1962	262	M

WM. LISTON, LTD.
Newhaven, Edinburgh

FUNNEL: *Yellow with black top and two blue bands. Hull: Blue with yellow line and red boot-topping.*

Admiral Rodney...	...	... A.199	1958	249	M
ex Star of Aberdeen—63					
Barbara Paton	...	...	... GW.7	1957	273	M
Gregor Paton	...	...	... GW.9	1958	273	M
Summerside	...	...	... LH.389	1960	217	M
Summervale	...	...	... LH.373	1960	217	M

J. LOVIE
Peterhead

Funnel:				Hull:		
Claben	...	...	...	1969	142	M

J. MARR & SONS, LTD.
Hull and Fleetwood

Funnel: *Red with black top.*   Hull: *Light brown with red boot-topping.*

Benella	...	...	...	...	H.132	1959	789	M
Brucella	...	...	...	...	H.291	1953	678	M
Corena	...	...	...	...	FD.173	1958	392	M
Criscilla*	...	...	...	...	FD.261	1966	952	M(A)
Dorinda	...	...	...	...	FD.22	1955	334	M
Edwina	...	...	...	...	FD.162	1958	392	M
Farnella*	...	...	...	...	—	1971	1,150	M
Gavina	...	...	...	...	—	1971	516	M
Irvana*	...	...	...	...	—	1971	532	M
Josena	...	...	...	...	FD.150	1957	392	M
Junella*	...	...	...	...	H.347	1962	1,435	DE
Kirkella*	...	...	...	...	H.367	1965	1,714	DE
Lancella	...	...	...	...	H.290	1953	790	SR
Luneda*	...	...	...	...	—	1971	—	M
Marbella*	...	...	...	...	H.384	1966	1,786	DE
Maretta*	...	...	...	...	FD.245	1965	439	M
Merrydale	...				—	1970	111	M
Northella*	...	...	...	...	H.301	1964	1,718	DE
Primella	...	...	...	...	H.98	1958	789	M
ex Northella–63								
Rosa Maris*	...	...	...	...	—	1970	111	M
Southella*	...	...	...	...	H.40	1969	1,144	M(A)
Starella	...	...	...	...	H.219	1960	606	M
Thornella	...	...	...	...	H.94	1955	793	SR
Velia	...	...	...	...	FD.116	1955	334	M
ex Collena–63								
Westella	...	...	...	...	H.194	1960	779	M
Zonia	...	...	...	...	—	1965	440	M
Dinas Steam Trawling Co. Ltd.:								
Arlanda	...	...	...	...	FD.206	1961	431	M
Dinas	...	...	...	...	FD.55	1956	440	M
Jacinta	...	...	...	...	FD.21	1955	334	M
Lucida	...	...	...	...	FD.237	1957	392	M

*Stern Trawler.

P. J. McLEAN
Aberdeen

Funnel:				Hull:		
Bickleigh	...	...	...	LT.444	1962	162	M

MINISTRY OF AGRICULTURE, FISHERIES & FOOD.
London

Funnel: *Yellow with black top.*   Hull: *Black with white line.*

Cirolana*	...	...	...	...	GY.156	1971	2,050	ME(A)
Clione*	...	...	...	...	LT.421	1961	495	M
Corella†	...	...	...	...	LT.767	1967	459	M(A)
Ernest Holt	...	...	...	...	GY.591	1948	604	SR

*Fishery Research Ship.   †Stern Trawler.

J. Marr & Sons Ltd.   M.T. BENELLA   [*John G. Callis*

Mitchell Bros. Ltd.   M.T. MERBREEZE   [*Port of Lowestoft Research Society*

Norrard Trawlers Ltd.   M. T. DAWN WATERS [*Port of Lowestoft Research Society*

MITCHELL BROS. LTD.
Lowestoft

FUNNEL: *As below.*   HULL: *Grey with white whalemouth.*

Jackora Ltd. (Funnel: Blue with white letter "H").

Jacklyn	...	...	...	LT.434	1962	165	M
Ocean Breeze	...	...	...	LT.341	1927	118	M

Norbreeze Ltd. (Funnel: Yellow with house flag).

Merbreeze	...	...	...	LT.365	1931	122	M

Mitchell's (Tritonia) Ltd. (Funnel: Blue with house flag).

Tritonia	...	...	...	LT.188	1930	123	M

Scattan Ltd. (Funnel: Yellow with house flag).

Hosanna	...	...	...	LT.167	1930	140	M

J. MUIR
Anstruther

FUNNEL: HULL:

Ocean Dawn	...	...	...	LT.466	1956	131	M

NEWINGTON TRAWLERS LTD.
Hull

FUNNEL: *Grey with black top separated by broad blue band.*   HULL: *Black with white line and red boot-topping.*

C. S. Forester*	...	...	...	H.86	1968	768	M
Ian Fleming	...	...	...	H.396	1958	598	M
ex Fylkir–66							
Joseph Conrad	...	...	...	H.161	1957	823	SR
Peter Scott	...	...	...	H.103	1957	666	SR
ex Primella–57	...	...					
Somerset Maugham	...	...	...	H.329	1961	789	M

*Stern Trawlers.

NORRARD TRAWLERS LTD.
Milford Haven

FUNNEL: *Yellow with blue star.*   HULL: *Grey with red boot-topping.*

Bryher	...	...	...	LT.371	1961	166	M
Constant Star	...	...	...	M.133	1962	136	M
Norrard Star	...	...	...	M.44	1956	167	M
Picton Sea Eagle	...	...	...	M.68	1958	197	M
Picton Sealion	...	...	...	M.22	1956	166	M
Rosevear	...	...	...	LT.457	1962	166	M

PUTFORD ENTERPRISES LTD.
Lowestoft

FUNNEL: *Black with orange band.* HULL: *Black.*

Ada Kerby	...	...	...	LT.72	1958	126	M
Bannockburn	...	...	...	KT.302	1957	178	M
ex Sutton Queen–71							
Dreadnought	...	...	...	A.377	1960	163	M
Idena	...	...	...	A.793	1953	317	M
Lord Keith	...	...	...	LT.481	1930	124	M
Mincarlo ...	...	...	...	LT.412	1961	166	M
Woodleigh	...	...	...	LT.240	1960	199	M

R. A. RAINBIRD
Newlyn

FUNNEL: HULL: *Grey.*

Yellowfin ...	...	...	...	LT.282	1945	115	M
ex Alorburn–52							

Norrard Trawlers Ltd. M.T. PICTON SEA EAGLE

[Port of Lowestoft Research Society

RANGER FISHING CO. LTD.
(G. R. PURDY)
North Shields

FUNNEL: *Black with broad white band.* HULL: *Black with white bulwarks and red boot-topping.*

Ranger Ajax*	...	...	...	SN.147	1965	778	M
Ranger Apollo*		...	...	SN.148	1965	778	M
Ranger Aurora*		...	...	SN.149	1966	779	M
Ranger Boreas*		...	...	SN.14	1963	928	M
ex Blankenese–70							
Ranger Briseis*		...	...		1962	982	M
ex Fritz Homann–70							
Ranger Cadmus*		...	...		1971	1,000	M
Ranger Calliope*		...	...		1971	—	M
Ranger Callisto*		...	...		1971	—	M
Ranger Castor*		...	...		1971	—	M

*Stern Trawler.

SIR THOMAS ROBERTSON & SON (GRIMSBY) LTD.
Grimsby

FUNNEL: *Black with red, white and blue tricolour flag.* HULL: *Black with red boot-topping.*

Ephesian	...	...	...	GY.604	1959	345	M
Galilaean	...	...	...	GY.603	1959	345	M
Judaean	...	...	...	GY.644	1961	275	M
Olivean	...	...	...	GY.92	1954	269	M
Philadelphian	...	...	...	GY.636	1961	275	M
Thessalonian	...	...	...	GY.112	1955	269	M
Tiberian	...	...	...	GY.673	1961	283	M

Onward Steam Fishing Co. Ltd.: (Black letter "O" on white of houseflag).

Rhodesian	...	...	...	GY.457	1957	331	M
Samarian	...	...	...	GY.445	1957	331	M

Dominion Steam Fishing Co Ltd.: (Black letter "D" on white of houseflag).

Priscillian	...	...	...	GY.672	1961	283	M

ROSS TRAWLERS LTD.
(BRITISH UNITED TRAWLERS GROUP)
Hull & Grimsby

FUNNEL: *Grey with black top and houseflag (White star on green ground).* HULL: *Black with red boot-topping.*

Ross Daring	...	...	...	GY.707	1963	201	M
Ross Fame	...	...	...	GY.1360	1965	457	M
Ross Fortune	...	...	...	GY.1365	1965	457	M
Ross Mallard	...	...	...	GY.699	1962	266	M
Ross Ramillies	...	...	...	GY.53	1950	747	M
ex Ross Fighter–66, Andanes–61							
Ross Resolution	...	...	...	GY.527	1948	564	M
ex Ross Stalker–66, Rinovia–60							
Ross Revenge	...	...	...	GY.718	1960	978	M
ex Freyr–63							

ROSS TRAWLERS LTD. *continued*

Ross Rodney	...	...	...	GY.34	1957	697	M
ex Rodney						
Ross Vanguard		...	...	GY.1372	1966	1,488	M

Queen Steam Fishing Co. Ltd.:

Ross Renown	...	...	...	GY.666	1962	790	M

Goweroak Ltd.:

Ross Cheetah	...	...	...	GY.614	1959	354	M
Ross Civet	...	...	...	GY.650	1960	352	M
Ross Cormorant	...		...	GY.665	1961	288	M
Ross Cougar	...	...	...	GY.531	1958	355	M
Ross Curlew	...	...	...	GY.692	1962	288	M
Ross Eagle	...	...	...	GY.656	1961	288	M
Ross Falcon	...	...	...	GY.667	1961	288	M
Ross Genet	...	...	...	GY.652	1960	352	M
Ross Hawk	...	...	...	GY.657	1961	288	M
Ross Heron	...	...	...	GY.693	1962	288	M
Ross Jackal	...	...	...	GY.637	1959	355	M
Ross Jaguar	...	...	...	GY.494	1957	355	M
Ross Juno ...	...	...	...	GY.660	1961	413	M
ex Padgett–65						
Ross Kandahar	...	...	...	GY.506	1958	507	M
ex Kandahar–62		...	...			
Ross Kashmir	...	...	...	GY.43	1957	489	M
Ross Kelly	...	...	...	GY.6	1956	489	M
ex Kelly–62						
Ross Kelvin	...	...	...	GY.60	1958	468	M
ex Kelvin–62						
Ross Kestrel	...	...	...	GY.658	1961	288	M
Ross Khartoum ...		...	...	GY.47	1958	507	M
ex Khartoum–62						
Ross Kipling	...	...	...	GY.38	1957	469	M
ex Kipling–62						
Ross Kittiwake		...	...	—	1961	288	M
Ross Leopard	...	...	...	GY.491	1957	355	M
Ross Lynx	...	...	...	GY.626	1960	354	M
Ross Panther	...	...	...	GY.519	1958	355	M
Ross Tiger	...	...	...	GY.398	1957	355	M
Ross Zebra	...	...	...	GY.653	1960	352	M

Charleson-Smith Trawlers Ltd.:

Ross Altair	...	...	...	H.279	1963	677	M
ex Stella Altair–65						
Ross Aquila	...	...	...	H.114	1956	780	M
ex Stella Aquila–65						
Ross Leonis	...	...	...	H.322	1960	775	M
ex Stella Leonis–65						
Ross Mallard	...	...	...	GY.699	1963	266	M
Ross Orion	...	...	...	H.235	1962	778	M
ex Stella Orion–66						
Ross Sirius	...	...	...	H.277	1963	677	M
ex Stella Sirius–65						

Ross Freezer Trawlers Ltd.:

Ross Implacable*	...		...	H.6	1968	1,042	M
Ross Intrepid	...	...	...	H.353	1965	1,156	DE
ex Ross Kennedy–66, Cape Kennedy–66						
Ross Valiant	...	...	...	GY.729	1964	1,156	DE

Hudson Bros. Trawlers Ltd.:

Ross Canaveral ...		...	...	H.267	1963	805	M
ex Cape Canaveral–66						
Ross Illustrious ...		...	...	H.419	1966	1,076	M
Ross Otranto	...	...	...	H.227	1962	823	M
ex Cape Otranto–66						
Ross Trafalgar	...		...	H.59	1957	787	M
ex Cape Trafalgar–66						

*Stern Trawler

PETER SLEIGHT TRAWLERS, LTD.
Grimsby

FUNNEL: *Black with blue letter "P" on white band between two blue bands.*   HULL:
Black with red boot-topping.

Fiskerton	GY.676	1962	199		M
ex *Balmoral–64*					
Kirmington	GY.1367	1960	226		M
ex *Admiral Cunningham–65, Star of Scotland–62*					
Scampton	GY.166	1961	214		M
Syerston	GY.1366	1960	226		M
ex *Admiral Ramsey–65, Star of the Isles–63*					
Waddington	GY.680	1962	230		M

SMALL & CO. (LOWESTOFT) LTD.
Lowestoft

FUNNEL: *Orange with house flag.*   HULL: *Blue.*

Roy Stevens	LT.271	1961	202		M
Suffolk Challenger	LT.555	1968	255		M
Suffolk Chieftain	LT.556	1968	255		M
Suffolk Craftsman	LT.422	1961	202		M
Suffolk Crusader	LT.557	1968	255		M
Suffolk Kinsman	LT.397	1960	202		M
Suffolk Mariner	LT.378	1961	202		M
Suffolk Punch	LT.395	1961	202		M
Suffolk Venturer	LT.777	1967	255		M
East Anglian Ice & Cold Storage Co. Ltd.:					
Constance Banks	LT.979	1967	255		M
Kittiwake Ltd.:					
Suffolk Endeavour	LT.789	1968	255		M
Suffolk Enterprise	LT.492	1957	245		M
ex *Imprevu–65, Boston Vanguard–62*					

STEVENSON & SONS, LTD.
Newlyn

FUNNEL: *Black with silver band.*   HULL: *Grey with red boot-topping.*

Elizabeth Ann Webster ...	PZ.291	1946	109		M
ex *Agnes Allen–62*					
Elizabeth Caroline ...	PZ.293	1946	112		M
ex *David Allen–62*					
Marie Claire	PZ.295	1946	112		M
ex *Elijah Perrett–62*					
St. Clair	PZ.199	1946	116		M
ex *Sabella–58*					

Also smaller vessels of under 100 g.r.t.

TALISMAN TRAWLERS LTD.
Lowestoft

FUNNEL: *Yellow with black letter "G".* HULL: *Black.*

Bentley Queen ...	...	...	LT.32	1971	—	M
Carlton Queen ...	...	...	LT.363	1961	196	M
Norton Queen ...	...	...	LT.356	1958	197	M
Ripley Queen ...	...	...	LT.30	1970	—	M
Underley Queen	...	...	LT.31	1971	—	M
Waveney Queen	...	...	LT.16	1968	239	M
Wilton Queen ...	...	...	LT.145	1960	199	M

Talisman Trawlers (North Sea) Ltd.:

Farnham Queen	...	...	LT.502	1961	246	M
ex Blacktail–65						
Oulton Queen ...	...	...	LT.503	1961	246	M
ex Dorade–65						
Yoxford Queen	...	...	LT.501	1962	246	M
ex Sailfin–65						

Talisman Trawlers Ltd.   M.T. CARLTON QUEEN

[Port of Lowestoft Research Society

BERNARD WILLIAMS & CO. LTD.
Swansea

FUNNEL:				HULL:		
Schiestroom	...	...	... M.202	1949	118	M

JAMES WILSON
Fleetwood and Buckie

FUNNEL: *Black with narrow blue band and separate monogram device.* HULL: *Black with white line and red boot-topping.*

Andrew Wilson M.73	1959	197	M
ex Virtue Pettit–68			
Georgina Wilson HL.10	1955	182	M
ex Fairy Cove–67			
Hazelglen BCK.145	1918	107	M
ex Castlebay–51, Dayspring			
Vigilance Fishing Co. Ltd.:			
Vigilance A.204	1958	149	M

J. M. WILSON
Anstruther

FUNNEL:			HULL:		
Suffolk Maid	... ... LT.295	1957	130	M

WOOD & BRUCE, LTD.
Aberdeen

FUNNEL: *Red with deep black top with varying additions of subsidiary coys.* HULL: *Black with white line and red boot-topping.*

Crusader Fishing Co. Ltd.:			
Red Crusader A.240	1958	274	M
Minerva Fishing Co. Ltd.:			
Alexander Bruce A.141	1957	274	M
David Wood A.142	1957	274	M
Strathcoe Fishing Co. Ltd.:			
Strathdon A.234	1958	275	M
Clova Fishing Co. Ltd.:			
Clova A.417	1961	281	M
Clovella A.63	1957	213	M
Wood & Bruce Ltd.:			
Glengairn A.491	1960	228	M
Glenisla A.282	1959	279	M

WOOD & LLEWELLYN
Milford Haven

FUNNEL: HULL:

Lord Suffolk	...	...	...	LT.44	1929	120	M
Roger Bushell	...	...	...	BM.76	1946	117	M

GEORGE WOOD (ABERDEEN) LTD.
Aberdeen

FUNNEL: *Cream with black top separated by narrow red band.* HULL: *Black with red boot-topping.*

Emma Wood	...	...	...	A.735	1947	197	M
ex Granton Kestrel–63, Teresa Watterston–58							
Silver Seas	...	...	...	A.65	1931	121	M
Ailsa Craig Fishing Co. Ltd.:							
George R. Wood		...	...	A.723	1919	209	M
ex Doreen Johnston–60, Adastral–46, William Gillett							
Netherley	...	...	...	A.465	1960	213	M
Strathallan	...	...	...	A.767	1956	181	M
Stratherrick	...	...	...	A.763	1960	237	M
Wilronwood Fishing Co. Ltd.							
Boston Sea Hawk	...	...	A.117	1953	180	M
Craiglynne	...	...	...	A.324	1960	163	M
Wilronwood	...	...	...	A.546	1961	166	M

THE JOHN WOOD GROUP (ABERDEEN) LTD.
Aberdeen

FUNNEL: *Black with black top with houseflag.* HULL: *Black with red boot-topping.*

Aberdeen Motor Trawlers, Ltd.:							
Aberdeen Enterprise	...		...	A.114	1957	266	M
Aberdeen Distributor	...		...	A.211	1958	281	M
Aberdeen Fisher		...	...	A.218	1958	245	M
Aberdeen Merchant	...		...	A.134	1957	284	M
Aberdeen Progress	...		...	A.157	1957	249	M
Aberdeen Venturer	...		...	A.488	1960	298	M
Admiral Hawke	...		...	A.520	1961	225	M
Admiral Nelson		...	...	A.469	1960	453	M
ex Princess Royal–63							
Admiral Vian	...	...	...	A.580	1961	226	M
ex Mannofield–62							
Ashley Fishing Co. Ltd.:							
Dalewood	...		...	...	A.481	1960	234	M
Japonica	...	...	...	...	A.524	1961	234	M
Jasmin	...	...	...	...	A.523	1961	234	M
Leswood	...	...	...	...	A.442	1960	237	M

THE JOHN WOOD GROUP (ABERDEEN) LTD. *continued*

Burwood Fishing Co. Ltd.:

Burwood ...	...	...	...	A.547	1961	249	M
Clarkwood	...	...	...	A.557	1961	249	M
Janwood ...	...	...	...	A.457	1960	250	M
Milwood ...	...	...	...	A.472	1960	250	M

Leslie Fishing Co. Ltd.:

Lorwood ...	...	...	...	A.400	1960	237	M
Marwood ...	...	...	...	A.306	1959	237	M
Starwood ...	...	...	...	A.431	1960	237	M

Wood & Davidson, Ltd.:

Peaceful Star ...	...	...	...	A.61	1931	121	M
ex Quiet Waters–49							

WYRE TRAWLERS, LTD.
(BRITISH UNITED TRAWLERS GROUP)
Fleetwood

FUNNEL: *Black with two narrow white bands.* HULL: *Black with white line and red boot-topping.*

Wyre Captain ...	...	...	FD.228	1953	490	M
ex Loch Melford–68, Prince Charles–57						
Wyre Conqueror	...	...	FD.187	1959	398	M
Wyre Corsair ...	...	...	—	1953	442	M
ex St. Claude II–68, Boston Javelin–53						
Wyre Defence ...	...	...	FD.37	1956	338	M
Wyre Gleaner ...	...	...	FD.269	1953	442	M
ex Saint Just II–57, Princess Anne–54						
Wyre Majestic ...	...	...	FD.433	1956	388	M
Wyre Revenge ...	...	...	FD.432	1956	338	M
Wyre Vanguard ...	...	...	FD.36	1955	338	M
Wyre Victory ...	...	...	FD.181	1960	398	M

Index

LATE CHANGES
ADDENDA

The fleets of the following companies are now incorporated in the newly formed **P. & O. Short Sea Shipping Ltd.** For the time being they continue to be operated by their erstwhile owners and retain their original colours. **Belfast S. S. Co., Burns & Laird Lines, Coast Lines Ltd., North of Scotland, Orkney & Shetland S. N. Co., Tyne-Tees Steam Shpg. Co., General Steam Navigation Co. Ltd.** and subsidiaries, and **North Sea Ferries, Ltd.**

Thun Tankers Ltd. has been acquired by **F. T. Everard & Sons, Ltd.,** and **Thuntank 5** and **Thuntank 6,** renamed **Amity** and **Anteriority** respectively, are now operated by **Thames Tankers Ltd.,** a subsidiary of the latter company.

Other new companies

H. L. Thompson (Shipholdings) Ltd., London

Channelbridge I	1970	373	223	43	10	M(A)
ex Malta Cross–72							

Sycamore Transporters Ltd., London

Acer	1956	554	191	31	12	M(A)
ex Commodore Clipper–72, Clipper–68